NOTES FROM
CHILDHOOD

NOTES FROM CHILDHOOD

Norah Lange

Translated by Charlotte Whittle

SHEFFIELD – LONDON – NEW YORK

First published in English in 2021 by And Other Stories
Sheffield – London – New York
www.andotherstories.org

Originally published in 1937 as *Cuadernos de infancia*
Copyright © Norah Lange, 1937
Translation copyright © Charlotte Whittle, 2021

9 8 7 6 5 4 3 2 1

ISBN 9781911508953
eBook ISBN 9781911508946

Editor: Bella Bosworth; Copy-editor: Robina Pelham Burn; Proofreader: Sarah Terry. Typeset in Linotype Swift Neue and Verlag by Tetragon, London. Cover design: Ronaldo Alves. Printed and bound on acid-free, age-resistant Munken Premium by CPI Limited, Croydon, UK.

This book has been selected to receive financial assistance from English PEN's PEN Translates programme, supported by Arts Council England. English PEN exists to promote literature and our understanding of it, to uphold writers' freedoms around the world, to campaign against the persecution and imprisonment of writers for stating their views, and to promote the friendly co-operation of writers and the free exchange of ideas. www.englishpen.org

And Other Stories gratefully acknowledge that our work is supported using public funding by Arts Council England.

Supported using public funding by
ARTS COUNCIL
ENGLAND

ENGLISH PEN

MIX
Paper from
responsible sources
FSC
www.fsc.org
FSC® C020471

CONTENTS

Flickering and joyous, broken by only a single night, the first journey we made from Buenos Aires to Mendoza emerges from my memory like a landscape recovered through a misted pane of glass.

My five years clung out of fear to the evening we arrived in Monte Comán, where we spent the night before continuing, the next morning, to our destination.

There were only a few rooms in the hotel, and all of us – my parents, Eduardito, the five girls, the governess, and the nanny – had to sleep in three cramped rooms, but neither this nor any discomfort could have diminished our excitement at the special occasion of having dinner with the grown-ups in the dining room of a hotel.

All five of us, in our white sailor dresses, awaited the moment so eagerly that our mother seemed to us to be dawdling as she got ready, and the nanny to be taking longer than ever to lull Eduardito to sleep.

When we finally entered the dining room, we saw a couple seated at the only occupied table. Soon after sitting down, we heard the waiter say to my father in a hushed tone, "That's the owner of the circus, and next to him is the strongest woman in the world. Every night she lifts three men with her teeth."

Five pairs of eyes, widened with curiosity, fixed on the couple all at once. I had my back to them, and had to twist around to stare at the woman. As I watched her, I thought I could see her body, her hideousness, expand little by little, and I was baffled that the circus owner could laugh, watch her eat, and sit so calmly by her side.

Across the table, my father told me to sit up straight, but before obeying I noticed the woman smiling at me, and since I wasn't brave enough to return the gesture, I turned around quickly and went on eating.

I had never been to the circus, and couldn't imagine that a woman might be able to dangle three men from her teeth. As I bent my head over my plate, the very idea caused an unstoppable wave of fear to rise up my legs. I thought the woman might be displeased that I hadn't returned her smile, and that, at the first opportunity, she would clamp me between her teeth. With my back to her, it was impossible for me to keep watch on whether she was getting up from her table and coming over to ours. Gradually, uncontrollably, my terror became so great that I almost burst into tears, and I begged my mother to let me sit beside her.

That night, to get to sleep, we had to wait until our fatigue had eclipsed the knowledge that the circus woman was staying in a room a short way from ours. The next morning, in two brakes – my parents, Eduardito, and the nanny in one; the governess and we five girls in the other – we set out for the neighboring town.

After a bumpy three-hour ride, we forded a stream. Before our brake plunged into the murky water, we looked – stricken – to the other one up ahead, seeking comfort from Mother, who, hunched over Eduardito, watched us closely as the horses splashed our white dresses and the water rose, almost covering the wheels' axles. We huddled together, trying to assuage our fear by stroking the dogs that cowered behind the seats. When we reached the other side, we felt the small joy that later would always be sparked by clods of mud flying from wheels and the light trot of horses after clearing a swampy and treacherous path.

Before darkness fell, we glimpsed the old house where we were to stay until the new one was built. A couple from San Luis welcomed us at the garden gate. The woman was wearing a dress with an immense floral train, which we assumed she must have dug out of a trunk to confer some grandeur on the occasion, but which, during the month and a half we stayed, she never removed.

At dinner time, we had to light a great many lamps and candles to watch the spiders and kissing bugs all over the walls. This didn't prevent us from jumping out of our skin at the slightest brush of a shoe against a chair, convinced that a mouse was climbing up one of our legs.

While we lived in the old house, we used to force ourselves to stay up until we were tired, so that when we went to bed we might drift off immediately and endure as briefly as possible our fear of the creepy-crawlies lurking there. During the day, after running around the land on the quinta, we climbed trees and clambered onto rooftops shrouded with creepers, in search of bats. If we managed to find one, we trapped it in a wire cage.

Motionless, hanging from the bars, they looked like dark, wrinkled rags. Sometimes, it seemed to us the bats were hiding their faces and weeping, so we would take them out of the cage and perch them on a branch so they could fly away.

At the time, I wasn't the least bit frightened or disgusted by them, but when we left that gloomy house – full of disjointed, mysterious spaces – and moved to the large house that was built for us, they clung so densely to the pale walls, and their flight was so silent, like a wet cotton drape flapping in an open window, that the very idea of them brushing against my cheek was enough for me to take a permanent dislike to them.

I see her framed with a gentleness no one could touch without taking something away, without adding more grace than that which was essential and true.

She used to ride her horse in one of those full, thick riding habits people wore in those days.

On one side of the horse, we saw the whole length of her, the black brim of her hat concealing her face. We saw only a single gloved hand on the other, yet her profile was as sharp as if she had suddenly drawn alongside a lamp.

From one flank of the horse, her whole body seemed to balance out the other, luminous side where her face could be fully seen. When she rode this way, our delight was doubled: we could see her from one side, the shadowy, mysterious side, while, from the other, where she was whole, we recovered her intact, identical to the picture of affection she showed every day.

To help her into the saddle, my father needed only to link his hands to lift her foot. Mother would mount, and once she was ready, immediately sit waiting attentively. Each of her movements, though new, soon formed part of a constant landscape.

My father would press his dapple-gray forward. When he tapped him lightly on the legs with his boot, the horse would stretch out his front and hind legs, crouching until the saddle was so low that my father no longer needed to use the stirrup.

Standing in a semicircle, my sisters and I would remark on the horse's meek and obedient nature. Then, after putting on this display, they would trot off slowly into the distance.

Our mother's radiant side would disappear, leaving only the one that was less familiar, more austere. As she approached the first poplars that bordered the quinta, we felt newly bereft. We could make out only my father's reddish beard.

Now I know that my mother's other side, the luminous one, rode close beside him.

Three windows look onto my childhood. The first belongs to my father's study. The few times we ever went into that room, we felt timid at the sight of the imposing furniture upholstered in cold, slick leather, and the walls covered in charts and maps of different countries. We sensed that one went there only to talk of serious things, or to dismiss a farmhand or a servant. The only thing I remember of my father's desk is the enormous globe he would sometimes spin to make Norway and Ireland suddenly appear before our eyes. A cabinet held a jumble of bows and arrows, pipes, and beads the native people had given him on his various expeditions, and which he allowed us to peek at from time to time.

At bedtime, we would glimpse a faint, almost imperceptible glimmer of light underneath his door. This was my father's writing time, and only Mother, with her enduring sweetness, might go in to speak with him.

When his window lights up suddenly and stands frozen in memory, it seems to possess the sorrow of unfinished letters, abandoned for some unknown reason, that one finds years later at the back of a drawer.

Mother's window was more inviting. It belonged to the sewing room. In houses with many children, the sewing room is always the sweetest, the most sought out. Beside sewing baskets overflowing with ribbons and lace, we often gazed upon little garments that weren't our size. We never suspected that someone else might arrive suddenly, after us. Mother spent hours on end in the sewing room, knitting and embroidering tiny things. She seemed more accessible there, more willing to let us unburden ourselves, so that when the youngest among us turned thirteen or fourteen, we understood that, in that room, it would have been easier to confide in her the fear, shame, ugliness, and sorrow of that awkward age. The three elder girls managed it. Susana and I were denied that tenderness: a window so tucked away, the light so perfect for hiding our blushing cheeks, the tears welling in our eyes, and our bitterness, our sense of being cut off from everyone by a contagious illness. Her window always had just the right light for children. I have never seen any such window since. Children arrive in rooms where no one awaits them, rooms that were not built with them in mind; their little clothes are sewn in bare courtyards, in bedrooms accustomed to other presences, affections, and memories, or at teatime, while chatting with visitors, in idle moments that do not allow for any devotion. I have seen so many women who do not alter their tone of voice, whose expressions remain unchanged, allowing jokes about their appearance or trying to disguise it, regarding life with neither more nor less concern, as if what they carried inside them weren't enough for them to see that theirs is the great joy of having a child; as if an imminent birth were part of the daily routine and there were no need to set aside days and nights for waiting, to be able to recall them later with an expression different from that used to speak of anything else.

My mother was different. My mother did not knit booties or blankets in idle moments. Idle time was made up of other things. Waiting, for her, was a duty, and she waited both day and night. When she entered that room suffused with warmth, it was as if her air, her expression, changed. Whenever I saw her withdraw to that room to sew such tiny things, she was wide-eyed and wistful from so much looking within, wearing a

13

gaze like one I've seen since in those who've been watching the sea. When we played in the garden, her lamp, whose light in winter was languid, reassured us of her presence. Little did we suspect that from one day to the next there might be another name in the house, another mouth to kiss before going to bed.

The third window was Irene's. I was always a little afraid and a little in awe of her. She was six years older than me. Sometimes, she was allowed to sit at the table in the large dining room during visits from family friends. My older sisters used to whisper about her. They had discovered her secrets, and spoke of these in a delighted, mysterious tone, far from believing that it would soon be their turn, too. Susana and I, the youngest two, weren't shrewd enough to guess the reason for these long whispering sessions. One afternoon, I heard them speak of breasts. When I think back, I understand the fear she must have felt – the first sister, all alone – when she saw her body begin to curve, her rib cage lose its rigidity, her breasts start to ache and stir imperceptibly.

From her window, we always awaited momentous surprises. Irene told us tales of kidnappings, of elopements, of how she would leave one morning with a knapsack like Oliver Twist, because she was unloved at home, or someone was waiting for her outside. Perhaps that's why, for me, her window was always mysterious.

One night, when we were all tucked in, Irene came to my bed to say farewell. Wrapped in a blanket, she had a bundle of clothes slung over one arm. She announced in a doleful voice that she was running away because we were so unkind to her and she was terribly miserable.

I thought straightaway of her window. I thought the moment had come. I got up and followed her, in tears. Much later, Marta's regretful lips told me it was all an act.

Then, little by little, her window faded away, until it looked just like the others.

She was four years older than me. We always seemed to come upon her long before the others, and it was as if she were always waiting for something.

She used to bite her lips until they bled, and slowly pick at the skin on her hands with her fingernails. In my memory, I still hold her in that pose, which always used to send a shiver down our spines: one hand open, the other always above it, moving so furtively that no one noticed her fingers delicately rubbing her already ragged skin, until, finally, a tiny trickle of blood caused by too tense a jerk would make her wince, only for her to return to silently tugging a less raw flap of skin, with a cautious, perfunctory hand.

I will always remember her hands. With their peeling skin, they looked like the pages of a well-loved book whose edges curl backward. I don't know how she could bear to touch anything, to brush against her clothes or against her own flesh. Unheeding, listless, and earnest, the world of her childhood held the intensity of one who waits, indifferent to what is to come.

Knowing she couldn't yet tell the time, my father made her study the clock each day. Marta would cry without sobbing, almost without any tears, covering her face with an open hand. Through the gaps between her outspread fingers, we could just make out a moistened eye, a patch of nose, a corner of mouth.

Once in a while, she shed her torpor and played alone. One night, she began to put on all the starched petticoats, adorned with the folds and ruffles people wore in those days. Little by little, her body began to swell, until her head was a tiny fair-haired dot atop an enormous crinoline. When Mother came into the room as she did every night to tuck her in, she found her asleep on her bed, exhausted, lost in a tangle of ribbons and lace.

The next morning at breakfast time, she wouldn't hear a single joke. She had recovered her serious, distant demeanor. One of her hands was stretched open beneath the table, the other slowly crawling between her fingers.

It could hardly have been easier to tell what she'd be like when she grew up.

Always willing to help with anything, she would follow Mother around the house and try to imitate her, until, gradually, she became like her in every way. When Mother was busy raking dry leaves in the garden, Georgina waited attentively to pick up the piles with a spade, so that Mother wouldn't have to take the trouble to ask. Sometimes we would go over and hint loudly that she was the favorite, so Mother would protest that she loved us all equally. Then, as if merely confirming a fact, we would add in a lower voice, "Not as much as you love Eduardito," since he wasn't just the only boy but also the youngest, and we suspected her affection would be unable to deny, with the same emphasis, so happy and natural a truth.

When I picture Georgina's immaculate, poised little figure, I can't help but compare her to one of those diligent children with perfect handwriting who cover their books with brown paper before they read them. She was so tidy she went as far as to sleep on her back, arms resting straight by her sides, so as not to wrinkle the sheets. Of the five girls, only she could be bothered to lay her clothes neatly across the chair when she undressed, and when we grew older, only she had a different dress for every occasion, an outfit for rainy days, and a light coat. The rest of us read in bed or sprawled in the first place we could find; Georgina sat up straight at her desk, resting only her arms. She won nearly all the prizes my parents awarded for good behavior and outstanding manners at the end of the year. She never put her elbows on the table – a sacrilege we often committed – and we were amazed by how she used the silverware with an ease that seemed, to the rest of us, so difficult to acquire.

One afternoon – she was barely seven – she insisted on operating the handle of the washing machine, a giant contraption with an octagonal drum for spinning and lathering the clothes, and two cylindrical rollers above for wringing and pressing the sheets and tablecloths. There was scarcely enough space between the rollers to feed in a tablecloth folded in four.

In an attempt to be helpful, Georgina fed the edge of a sheet between the two rollers. The washerwoman turned the handle, but didn't notice the fingers that hovered too close. We heard a shriek. In her confusion, the woman couldn't turn back the handle, until Mother, out of her wits, frantically pushed her aside and pulled it back in the other direction. Only then could Georgina remove her hand; I imagined her bones would be crushed to dust, her hand as flat and white as an unworn glove.

Georgina wailed in untold despair as they readied the cart to take her to the pharmacy in town. From a short distance, I watched her sobs unravel her tidy, upright figure for the first time. As my sisters tried to console her, somebody elevated her hand.

Before she got into the brake, it seemed to me that I should get closer. I was afraid my sisters might think it odd of me to hang back, or that I didn't feel as sorry as they did; but ever since I was small, whenever anything serious has befallen those close to me, I have never been able to free myself of the uneasy sense that nothing I do or say will go unnoticed, that someone is always watching me. Later, I realized we were all the same.

When I resolved to move closer, I did so with terrible fear, and once I was near, I looked at her finger. It was impossible to see the mark of the rollers, the flattened finger I imagined severed from her hand. Everything had been darkened by blood. When I saw this, I was almost happy, since that way her pain didn't hurt me as much.

Ever since I was very little, I have liked to watch people closely. By the time I was six years old, the habit had already taken root. Then I would laugh; I laughed so much that Mother used to warn guests I was terribly "cheeky." Although in English the word can mean insolent, I know it was neither insolence nor ill will, since the habit stayed with me until I was older and able to study it.

Whenever I fixed my gaze on the people who came to see us – the parish priest, the town doctor, the Bishop of Such and Such, and all the visitors who stayed at our house – I would imagine their profile from within. It was as if I had physically entered a person, but only their face. At the sight of a hunchback or someone missing a limb, I never felt the urge to recreate their figure with my own body. But their profile . . . ! Those quiet profiles with suddenly a curve for every tear: profiles always glimpsed through a misted pane of glass, faces that seem made especially to attract flies. Why should flies always land on the face of someone unloved . . . ? Or is it just that they go unnoticed on the faces of those who are dearer to us?

At the age of six, whenever I noticed a pronounced curve in the nose of any of the important men who filed through my house, I would laugh. Then I would slide into their faces, positioning my body inside to adjust to their silhouette.

Sometimes, I found myself kneeling with my arms outstretched: this was the parish priest's face with his straight, elongated nose and faintly defined eyebrows. At other times, I stepped inside the head doctor's face. Then I would have to sit cross-legged to shape his broad nose; the tips of my toes were enough to sketch his mouth, which was barely there, and my folded arms were his tiny eyes.

Bok, the engineer with a square and reddish beard, called for a greater sacrifice. I had to settle in upside down for my hair to form his beard, my hands barely clasped behind my back, my legs folded, forming an obtuse angle with my body, to imprint the slight tension onto his eyes that raised his eyebrows higher than normal.

This pastime lasted several years. Later, someone told me that people are known by their faces, and when I confessed that I always tried to slip into the faces of others, they answered me gravely that a face should say everything from the outside. But I paid them no heed, since that didn't seem very entertaining.

One afternoon – by then, I was eleven – I wanted to go inside a face and shape someone's features with my body. I had to make many imaginary figures, many limp arms and tangled legs. When I managed it, the result was so terrible that I was afraid.

Two months later, the person in question died. I imagined them inside their coffin in the position I'd arranged for them, which had been like a premonition.

From then on, whenever I looked at a stranger, out of habit my body would slowly contort so I could slip into their face; but the game no longer brought me satisfaction, nor any joy, and in the end, I abandoned it.

When Susana turned four, a serious illness deprived her of the use of her legs, and only some time later did she learn how to walk again. Always in a foul temper, she was enraged by the slightest thing; each time the doctor listened to her heartbeat there was a struggle, and whenever he begged her to stick out her tongue she would make him wait, and when she did comply, she would roll it up and make it impossible to examine.

At breakfast time, all of us hung on her mood.

"I want to cry!" she would suddenly shriek, and no matter how anyone rushed to prevent it, she would burst into inconsolable sobs. Mother would calm her down by moistening the back of her neck with a sponge.

"Now I want to laugh!" And our faces would soon relax at this pleasing change.

"Now I want to cry!" And on and on, for two or three months we put up with the changing weather of her moods, not saying a word. Any annoyance did so much harm that we had no choice but to obey her. But we couldn't cry for no reason, and could often scarcely hide our impatience before her dreadfully wide blue eyes and her unruly, flaming hair.

While she was bedbound, she continually asked for the governess.

"I want Lala!" This was how she shortened Miss Whiteside's mysterious, familiar name.

When Lala appeared, she would demand with a scream that she leave, repeating her order in the same ungodly tone at one, two, and three in the morning, until she fell asleep. Without the slightest impatience, with unwavering gentleness, the governess always came when she called.

"Put my doll over there! Now put it back! I don't want to see you! Go away! Go away right now! I want to cry!"

Miss Whiteside would leave. After two nights of this dreadful task, she opted to sit behind a screen, and would just be dozing off when the voice gave its order again from the bed.

"I want Lala!"

Miss Whiteside would appear from behind the screen and then, when the order was reversed, slip away on her rubber heels to try and sleep in her hiding place.

With heavy, unhurried hands, as if his whole life rested on one of his gestures, he moved his arms one by one, until he had to move both to pick something up. Whenever he embraced anyone, his right arm arrived a moment later, as if at first faltering, then rushing to stress the affection, full of regret. When he asked for a glass of water, he didn't gulp it all down like the others, but took little sips, removing the glass from his mouth, as if savoring the taste of the water each time he swallowed. If he had to say the word "very" – "very hot," "thank you very much" – he would make an astonished, defensive expression, then repeat under his breath, "Very, very."

Once, a fly settled silently on his bare arm. Both of us saw the insect, but I thought it strange that he didn't swat it, and waited a few minutes to see what would happen. Suddenly, in the quavering voice of someone on the verge of tears, he said, "Go away, little girl. I think your mother is calling you . . . " I thought he wanted to eat the fly.

He lived in a room near our quinta, and was called upon whenever the fruit needed picking or the trees pruning. When he chopped off a branch, he would gaze at it for a while, and then, averting his eyes, would let it fall. No matter how anyone hinted that he should work more quickly, he would pretend not to notice, making the excuse that the tree was blighted and he had to be thorough.

One afternoon when he fell asleep beside a gate, I tiptoed toward him and grazed his face and neck with a branch, so he would think it was an insect. He woke as if he'd been dreaming of sorrowful things, and as I laughed a little awkwardly, he stood up and brushed his head with his hand.

"I was in my house while you were laughing, little girl. Thank you very much." He repeated "very" under his breath, then went on his way.

After that, he never worked on our quinta again.

In wintertime, two or three times a week, Miss Whiteside would take us out for a walk.

We would be dressed identically: a blue skirt, red or green knitted sweater, and matching cap. Before we reached the town, the governess would urge in her plummy English, "Remember your blue blood, and behave accordingly." But as the five of us walked down Avenida del Nevado, surrounding the governess, her proud advice did nothing to prevent people from pointing and saying, "Here comes the red family, the green family . . . "

At other times we wandered down a wide dirt avenue still known today as Algarrobo Bonito, which always gave off a scent of damp earth. But one afternoon, when she noticed our undue interest in the view on that route, Miss Whiteside decided we wouldn't walk all the way to the end, with the excuse that we'd already gone far enough.

Beyond the carob tree that gave the avenue its name lay a cluster of ramshackle houses, whose inhabitants spent most of the day in their doorways facing the street. In front of one of these dwellings, we always used to see a tiny creature lying in a wooden crate scarcely larger than a shoebox.

The first time we saw her lying down in the crate, we imagined she was playing at being a doll. Little children scurried around and leaped over her, and neither the slightest surprise nor distress could make her sit up.

We saw her many times, and became intrigued by her insistence on staying inside the crate. Though she looked very weak and exhausted, we couldn't understand how a child – one of only two years at the most – should cling to such an odd custom.

One day, we learned the truth. Despite appearances, she was four and a half years old, but had stopped growing suddenly at fifteen months. Two years had now gone by, and no change could be seen in her. When her parents discovered that it calmed her down, and that it so entertained her to watch the children and people who passed in the street, they placed her next to the doorstep, in a crate so she wouldn't fall, and since she seemed to like it, when the afternoon bustle began on Avenida del Algarrobo, they took her out to the path in her little crate.

Marta had peritonitis two years after we arrived in Mendoza, and during her convalescence, the doctor advised her to sun-bathe for longer and longer each day.

We would see her spend interminable hours on the terrace after lunch with a resignation that was in fact extreme ill temper, her legs covered by a blanket and her clothing hitched up to her waist, her naked belly the color of toast.

We watched her do this every day for two or three months. Often, we would chant, "Brown belly, brown belly," just to annoy her. She was so embarrassed and weak that she couldn't muster an answer, and would start to cry and make strange, mute expressions of a kind I have never seen in another child.

One afternoon, we heard her murmur in a low voice:

"God is evil. God is evil . . . "

She had just turned ten, and this phrase, which seemed deadly serious in itself, left a far greater impression when we realized she was saying it over and over in a firm, decisive, urgent voice.

Later, she told me that for a long time she had felt so wretched that "God is evil" was all she could manage to say. She had to say it aloud, as if in defiance of someone. Even if only fleetingly, the phrase made her ten years seem as dreadful as if a child were waiting for dark to say to himself, "My mother is evil, my mother is evil," over and over and all alone, and

I thought such ill temper and fatigue could never be cloaked in forgetfulness.

Once, when I heard her from my room as she sunbathed, I was about to say, "Brown belly, brown belly," slowly from behind the door. But I felt a little ashamed when I saw her lips move softly, so no one would notice that she was talking to herself.

"God is evil."

This obsession pursued her for a long time. Years later, when we spoke of it, I was relieved to know that, even so, she still prayed each night like the other sisters.

Each day, Miss Whiteside gathered us in the schoolroom to continue our lessons in English, geography, history, and religion. My sisters studied diligently. Susana and I didn't begin until later, and I still remember the first things I read in a book about Manet. We learned very little about Argentina.

In the afternoons, while my sisters practiced scales on the piano or learned to darn socks with those big wooden eggs hardly used anymore, I would sit on the floor and entertain myself with my favorite pastime. With a pair of scissors, I would clip words from the local and foreign papers, arranging them into little piles. Most of the time, I didn't know what they meant, but I didn't mind this at all. What drew me in was the typeface, the thick and thin strokes of the script. Words in capital letters, like TWILIGHT, DISCOVERY, DAGUERROTYPE, LABYRINTH, and THERAPEUTIC, brought me a zeal and contentment all by themselves that now I would have to describe as aesthetic. Their intimate, expressive, mysterious quality – the visions that might lie behind some of them – didn't stir the slightest interest in me. I clipped them out purely for the tricky sonority of the more unusual words, those I was always most drawn to, that existed as if apart from the rest. Tangled letters, and the stiff downstrokes of the *l*s and *t*s, offered me more distraction than a game of patience.

As I played my game of typographic solitaire, and heard the names of Nelson, Napoleon, and Wellington – scarcely ever the name of an Argentine hero – I unconsciously acquired a mistaken belief in words themselves, in their apparent beauty, a beauty that reaches its fullness only behind, within itself.

Across the way from our quinta lay a cluster of houses and a small hut whose patched-up walls of crumbling adobe barely managed to keep it standing. One day, a man and a woman came to the hut so destitute that, when they took shelter there, they didn't even have anywhere to sit until Mother sent over some food and clothing and two wicker hanging chairs. The woman rarely left the hut, but when she did, we would glimpse her figure hunched over in the distance, an old shawl always wrapped around her shoulders. Later, we learned that she was consumptive, and that her husband barely managed to scrape together a few pennies by doing minor carpentry jobs.

One afternoon, we learned that Andrea was on her death-bed. When the news traveled that she had died, we saw her husband call at the garden gate. We assumed he would want some help with the burial or some more flowers, but he had only come to ask for a safety pin to fasten his shirt. He thought it improper to mourn with his neck exposed, and, on the death of his wife, this was the only change in dress that he could afford.

It seemed dreadful that he should ask for nothing more than a safety pin.

When my father went to see him, he found him alone in the room, standing before the body he'd wrapped in a sheet and laid in the coffin himself. Two plain candles illuminated her head. The light fell onto the lane through the ruined window, and filled with dust.

The next morning, very early, we heard the blows of a hammer. It was the man from across the way, nailing the coffin shut. We pictured him alone in the room, working as usual, a fistful of nails in his mouth as he lowered the lid, covering the ravaged body he knew so well.

By noon, a cart had come from town and taken the body away.

I believe no case of poverty has touched me so much since then.

The townspeople, neighbors, guests, and anyone passing through would always remark on his sweet face, curls, and immense blue eyes. Until the age of five, he was a perfect child, and from the time he was a baby, my older sisters would hover around him so Mother would let them change him, lull him to sleep, or hold him in their arms.

One night, my parents went out for a while, leaving Eduardito in the care of the nanny, who withdrew to her room after tucking him in. As he lay in his crib next to Mother's bed, his cries could be heard all the way in our rooms. Before going to bed ourselves, we went in to see him, and the astonishment in his huge, dreamy blue eyes beneath the mosquito net stayed with us a while until we went to sleep.

Perhaps, that night, he sensed that the huge bed was empty. He was used to someone coming in right away, and his small cries swelled to a desperate, urgent pitch. My sisters said from their beds that he shouldn't be up so late, and that it might be harmful for him to cry so much. The two eldest decided to rise, and, as always, we followed them.

One by one, in our nightgowns, we went into Mother's room. Irene thought there was no need to wake the nanny, so she asked us to go back to bed; she would calm him down, and so that Marta wouldn't blame her for taking advantage of being the eldest, she promised to call her if he didn't fall asleep soon.

From our beds we heard his persistent, monotonous cries, until a long silence suddenly fell. Fifteen minutes went by. In the end, when Irene didn't come back, Marta's impatience convinced us to find out why.

We tiptoed across the landing and peeked into Mother's room. Irene sat on the bed with an air of mystery and sacrifice, holding Eduardito in her arms. Her unfastened nightgown revealed a bare breast. She was only thirteen, and though they had sometimes walked in on her half-undressed, our sisters had never seen more than a gentle curve, the source of so many whispers and teasing remarks. We saw in amazement that she held her hand just as Mother did, gently lifting her small, round breast, on which Eduardito rested his mouth.

We left the room, resentful, perhaps unconsciously repulsed. Irene seemed all of a sudden grown-up.

We had made large hats out of paper. The five of us, standing in front of the mirror, each pausing before her own face, gazed at the effect of the shadow over our eyes, the contrasting glimmer of the light coming through the window as it glanced off our hair, against the newspaper.

Suddenly, the door opened, and a gust of air made the hats flutter on top of our heads.

One of my sisters said, "The first one to lose her hat will die before the others . . . "

Frozen in front of the mirror, arms linked so that no one could cheat, we played at who would be first to die.

A terrible fear slowly took hold of me. The open door let in a quick, threatening breeze that any moment might snatch away my hat. I thought of Irene, Marta, Georgina, Susana, and myself, and as I stole sideways glances, smiling along with them, a dead woman of twenty lay across the face of each of my sisters; a perfect, dead young woman, with a single flower on her pillow.

The wind shook the large paper triangles, without toppling them.

Georgina, her eyes fixed on some dreadful vision like mine, cried abruptly, "I hate these games!" and, stepping away from the mirror, took off her hat, crumpled it up, and flung it onto the floor.

For a while, the row of heads in front of the mirror conjured probable, sorrowful images, faces eternally mourned, and it seemed it would have been better to wait for the wind to predict the nearest death, so we could be sweeter and gentler to the sister who would be first to die.

From the time I turned four, the people around me would often say, "She may not be pretty, but what lovely hair she has! She looks like a boy." Back then, I didn't mind their remarks, and when someone stroked my head and said I looked like a little boy, I naively believed it was meant as a compliment.

One afternoon, I was called out onto the terrace. The commission agent, to whom we always entrusted the shopping in Buenos Aires, was waiting, loaded with boxes and packages. I assumed they must have bought me a new dress to wear on Sundays, when the governess took us to the Club or for a stroll down Avenida del Nevado.

When I stepped onto the terrace, everyone seemed to be hiding something. I noticed my father had a little glint in his eye, the glint we would always see when he was feeling free of cares. Then I saw my mother trimming ribbons and straightening bows, and trying on a wide-brimmed hat.

My father took me in his arms and stood me up on the table. My sisters had already looked through everything, and I felt slightly afraid since they seemed to expect something from me, and from whatever was hidden in the box Mother was unwrapping at that very moment.

I was always dressed in a pair with Susana – they bought different clothes for Irene, and dressed Marta and Georgina identically – so I was surprised that she wasn't on the table, too.

Once Mother had untied the box, I saw her remove a dark suit made of heavy fabric. Someone took off my pinafore, then made me lift one leg after the other. I was used to sticking my head through a hole when putting on a dress, and this new method made me as cross as I was at my sisters' gleeful mood. I thought they were dressing me up in a costume, and I couldn't imagine why they would have chosen me, the ugliest one.

When the suspenders were fastened they added a jacket, then left me standing all alone on the table.

"Now she really does look like a little boy!" Mother cried, as my sisters surveyed the results of this new attire and smiled in approval.

My eyes began to sting and I suddenly felt ridiculous and abandoned. I thought they were planning to put me on display. Little by little, the first rebellious, indignant sob rose up inside me. I didn't want to cry. It seemed absurd to cry dressed up as a man, so, instead, I let out a shriek.

"I don't want to be a boy! I don't want to be a boy!"

My mother took me in her arms to remove the strange new clothes. I cried so much my despair seemed more like a nervous breakdown. Worried, full of regret, my mother stroked me, while the others hid the suit and took away their things as if ashamed. The episode was never mentioned again.

Our favorite place on Avenida del Nevado was the cinema, where we went only when a circus was having a matinée. Whenever we passed by, we would stop to look at the posters, and long to be allowed into that room, at the moment it filled with a thick and mysterious darkness we sensed would be unlike any other we'd known.

One afternoon when a comedy was being shown, Mother finally decided to allow us to see a film.

When we returned, our excitement surpassed all expectations. We talked about everything: the tables by the seats where they served tea and big dishes of fried potatoes; our subtle shiver when the lights went down and we couldn't tell where Miss Whiteside was; the marvelous moment when the screen lit up and we saw a woman floating toward us, gazing at us all the while.

That night, to celebrate the occasion, we were allowed to dine with the grown-ups and we stayed on the terrace past the usual hour.

But suddenly, our voices ceased to carry the sound of festivities through the house. The thud of hooves echoed monotonously along the road, and an urge we couldn't have explained propelled us toward the gate. A dapple-gray horse loped by, his head bent low and his reins hanging loose. On his back rode a man, though we couldn't tell who, since the brim of his hat obscured his face. For a few seconds, the light from our gate fell on him in a slant. We saw a bundle laid across the horse's rump. It was the body of a dead man. He lay facedown across the animal, arms dangling mournfully from one side, legs from the other, until his listless swaying slowly entered the shadow that seemed to await him.

My memory of the first film we ever saw is always shot through with that of a lone man on the road to the town cemetery.

Usually, Marta would make up her own games, and almost never let us participate. When she entertained herself alone with something new, she had the look of a child who plays as if out of obligation, as if predicting the grown-ups' urging, the surprise in their faces at the unheard-of spectacle of a child not wanting to play, who would rather sit quietly at home in a corner or peer out of an open window.

The two things I remember most about her as a child are her peeling hands and her stubbornness when we would put on a play. When the governess made us learn a children's sketch, Marta always raised objections as soon as the roles were assigned. To banish any suspicion of favoritism, Miss Whiteside would give the starring role to Irene, the second to Marta, and so on. We accepted the part that fell to us without complaint. Marta, on the other hand, couldn't bear to be cast in a role that lacked grandeur and beauty, that wasn't swathed in distinction, and, before accepting a supporting role, would put up a fight as serious as the one caused by *Snow White*, when she wanted to play only the hushed but sentient lady lying in her coffin made of glass.

One afternoon I remember, as we finished a game of croquet, we saw her wander off toward the corral where the goats were kept. We were sure she was going to invent a new game, and since she was taking a long time to come back, we decided to see what was going on. When we reached the gate, we saw her closely inspecting the ground as a wide-eyed nanny goat stared at her in astonishment.

"Do you want to see what I'm doing?" she asked, brandishing a stick which at first she'd managed to hide. Not waiting for us to answer, she approached the friendliest goat and lifted its tail with one hand, while with the other she inserted one end of the stick. The nanny goat sprang up into the air and then, recovering from its fright, scattered the ground with little black droppings. Marta laughed, and we saw that the corral was littered with them.

"I still have two left to do," she announced, as if thoroughly pleased with her success thus far. But, outraged, we had already left.

I'll never be able to forget it, since my finger still bears a white mark that hums with static whenever it brushes against anything.

I was eight years old. One morning, I tried to slice through a loaf of bread, one of those loaves with slightly raw dough in the middle, which my sisters and I all loved equally. The knives had just been sharpened, and the bread knife, with its serrated edge, complicated the simple operation of slicing.

Someone snatched the knife away from me. I grasped at it stubbornly, but my hand arrived a little too late, and instead of the handle, met the knife's sharp, undulating blade. One of my sisters tugged at it. As my fingers slipped along its edge, I felt as if something hot had been left on the knife. I soon realized that this was the pain, and that, as it left my hand, the blade had sliced open my ring finger to the bone.

Despite my having to keep it bound to my chest for several weeks, when they removed the bandage, the whitish scar looked more alive than ever.

After a while I began to forget about it, began to provoke less often the kind of electric current I experienced when rubbing it, which gave me a strange and pleasant sensation.

One night around the New Year, we were allowed to drink some champagne. I wanted to feel sad, since I thought it fitting to drink and be sad. When I went to bed, a little less tired than usual, for a long time I lay there, thinking of tragic, ailing women, their hands stretched out on a quilt, or sitting beside a window. But my bed seemed to be tilting to one side.

I can't remember if, when I touched the scar by accident, I gave it the nervous tap I'd neglected for a long while, which caused a shiver to run down my arm like a dog repeatedly licking the palm of a hand. A sudden tingling seemed to lift the finger away from the others, and the tingling to translate into a word: "Itilínkili." I thought I had misunderstood, and as I gently lifted my hand, I saw the finger rise to gaze at me as it said, "Itilínkili."

"Itilínkili" seemed to imply a reproach or a grievance, since I didn't keep watch on the finger every day. Itilínkili, itilínkili . . . I heard it say over and over until I fell asleep with the sense that it was still standing, all through the night, telling me of its woes.

After that, whenever I drank a little, I would see it stand to attention to tell me its word. One night, it grew weary. I no longer hear it anymore. Itilíkili, itilínkili . . .

When Georgina was one – Susana and I weren't born yet – the nanny who pushed her around the plaza in her little pram gave her a branch with which to entertain herself. In a careless moment, Georgina swallowed one of the leaves. Years later, Mother would describe her distress as she thought she was dying.

By dint of habit and mischief, the older sisters convinced her that she still carried it inside, and that no sooner than the leaf found a tree to which it belonged, it would stir lightly and rise up into her mouth, and the wind would place it on one of the branches. For this to happen, she needed to know from which kind of tree it came, to go near the trees on the quinta so the leaf could spy them from its hiding place. Otherwise, a new tree would grow inside her.

Fearful and hesitant, Georgina wandered among the trees, leaning against the thick trunks, contemplating the foliage, as if waiting for something rare and mysterious to happen.

From time to time, the sisters would approach and ask, "Can you feel something? Is anything moving inside?" and as Georgina touched her throat, shaking her head, she would say, "It must be that one, or the one near the gate. They don't have very big leaves . . . "

Susana and I were terrified and followed her around, thinking how dreadful it would be if a tree grew straight up inside her.

When the sisters tired of teasing her, they decided to make her believe a tree had just recognized the leaf, and she no longer needed to wait for it to rise into her mouth, since the leaf would fly to its tree by night as she slept, and she would never know a thing about it.

The next morning, we had scarcely sat down to breakfast when Marta asked, "How are you? Do you feel better now that you don't have a leaf inside?"

But Georgina laughed. She had already cried in Mother's arms.

When the saltpeter dried the earth and gave it a muted, pallid look, it broke the earth into pieces of different shapes that curled slightly upward. Sometimes the five of us, as we kneeled in the road, piled up big pieces of this fragmented, hardened dirt that held together despite its cracks as long as we slid our hands underneath, lifting it cautiously from its place.

How many times, walking among the poplars, did I avoid stepping on one of those enormous tiles of earth with white edges and deep, precise cracks that lay on the road, like huge lily pads growing in ponds.

Before scratching our names with a stick, we would pick up some of the pieces that made up an endless game of patience, and arrange them in a row with the utmost care. If one of these little dry islands broke in our hands, we crumbled it into dust so it wouldn't be left alone and could again become part of the road. Just beneath, we found softer earth that could be stirred around, on which we would scratch the letters in a name.

When we crossed the town plaza we would see countless mosaics of broken earth, pushed aside and forgotten beneath the benches, as if their ash-edged presence or their distracting cracks had made someone impatient. For a while I assumed it was due to shoes grazing the ground, to the coming and going of people who sat on the bench. Now I know it was the pairs of lovers who pushed them aside so they could write, like us, on the fresh earth they covered, the name that was most familiar and most dear. When I noticed an impatient foot piling them into a mound beneath the bench or behind a tree, a strange tenderness made me avert my eyes, and I knew that if nobody else were there, I would have sprinkled them over the path to rid myself of the urgent need to prevent something from being left alone.

When I think of the house in Mendoza, more than the trees, more than the landscape, I am met with those pieces of earth that lay in the road like great motionless leaves the wind failed to sweep away, and my memory piles them into a mound again beside a bench, behind a tree, so their hardness will do no harm to such a sweet and sorrowful calligraphy.

After lunch, we would hear a rustle like the sound made by horses munching on corn. It was the wheels of the cart on the gravel. Pascual, the driver, would announce that the brake was ready, and after a half-hour journey, the five of us would reach the quinta of our French teacher, Madame Lagrange, whose elegance and refinement we still recall to this day.

Madame Lagrange always welcomed us like guests, and though we went to her house four times a week, her fresh welcome never became routine, and she never showed any sign of having greeted us just the same way two days earlier.

Her fifteen-year-old daughter Jacquette had thick, dark braids that hung down her chest, and I was full of admiration for her. Yet this admiration was fitful, since I admired her only in memory. When I observed her up close as she helped us out of our coats, or served the cinnamon milk we loved so much, my admiration dwindled to near indifference, and I would have preferred to see her less, and for someone to tell me stories in which she played a part.

In those days, I was convinced that women should be physically feeble, and that a kind of languor, a perpetual convalescence, was the epitome of true femininity. Certain that a woman who fainted often was perfect, I lay down one night with a hand at my throat, imagining myself unconscious. Anxious to become an ideal woman, I abstained from breathing and, closing my eyes halfway, waited for the ceiling and walls to start sweetly spinning around me and for the sudden feeling that I was about to faint. But that night, I fell asleep sooner than ever.

One afternoon at teatime, Madame Lagrange told us not to wait for Jacquette, since she had fainted while being fitted for a dress. As soon as I heard the word fainted I paid attention, certain I'd finally find myself in the presence of a perfect woman. When my older sister asked if she was seriously ill, I was left in suspense, fearful it might be something unusual, in which case my interest would have been less. To my great relief, the teacher went on in an unworried tone, "She always faints when she's fitted for a dress. She can't stand for long without doing anything, and no matter how quickly the seamstress works, as soon as she asks her to hold out an arm, she has to lie down and be fanned. The same thing happens at school. I've had to ask them not to make her stand when she takes her tests."

My admiration, utterly convinced, lacked only one more surprise for its delight to be complete. I had to see her swoon in just the way I had pictured, awash in shades of pallor, hands moving over a curtain, clinging to the back of a chair, unable to grasp them firmly. I resolved to beg the teacher to let me spy through a crack in the door the next time she had a fitting, but gave up on the idea for fear of my sisters' disapproval.

When Jacquette came into the dining room, a little pale, I couldn't stop staring at her. My sisters spoke and helped her as if she were an invalid. Her eyes seemed veiled by a trace of darkness, and the veins on her neck and hands, more prominent than ever, throbbed almost imperceptibly.

When we took our leave, she hurried to gather our things as usual and pass us our coats. Everyone insisted she stay still and no one would let her help. I hesitated a moment. Affecting absentmindedness, I allowed her to hold my coat, and, though

I knew it was heavy, I slipped my arms in slowly, hoping that if she exerted herself she might faint again.

She fainted three times that winter alone. To get her strength up, she was made to eat heartily, to exercise, and to ride. Nothing seemed so silly to me as imposing a regime to cure her anemia, and whenever she turned down a second glass of milk or a slice of toast, her poor appetite helped me recover my certainty that she was utterly feminine.

Once, the teacher mentioned her calmly, in a tone that seemed not to bode well. My fear of hearing something unpleasant urged me to leave the room, but I refrained since I was sure the teacher would think it impolite. With resignation, I prepared to hear as little as possible.

"Jacquette is much better. She faints less and less often now, and the doctor assures us that soon she won't faint at all."

When Jacquette came into the dining room, her pale face failed to excite me. I had lost interest. Now, she was no different from us.

Georgina was ill. Mother had to go constantly into her dimly lit room, almost on tiptoes, to change the cool cloths that covered her brow, while in the next room we tried to make as little noise as possible. Weary of our involuntary confinement, we decided to go outside and play catch. When we came near the poplars, I noticed Susana wasn't among us, and decided to go off in search of her. As I went into the salon, I heard someone coming and hid behind a door with the intention of giving her a fright. I was about to burst out when I noticed Susana was walking on tiptoe and pouting, and had something hidden in her hand. I assumed she'd been scolded, and waited for her to pass by so I could follow.

Once she had made sure no one was there, she went to Georgina's room, slowly walked to her bed, and removed the cloth from her brow. Then she held out the little mound of wet ribbon in her hand, placed it on Georgina's forehead, and left the room in the same silent, mournful way she had entered.

I tiptoed carefully over to the bed. Georgina was dozing. On her pale brow, I saw a blue ribbon. It was Susana's favorite ribbon, the great big bow Mother tied in her curls when she wanted her to look especially elegant.

Irene must have been about fourteen when we all came down with typhoid fever.

I always enjoyed getting sick. If at breakfast time Mother touched my brow and asked me to take my temperature, I would monitor her expression, as I handed back the thermometer, for any change that might give me the joy of knowing I'd have to stay in bed. If, on top of this, it rained in the afternoon, my happiness would be complete, since I knew my mother and sisters would come to my room and sit at the foot of the bed, and that everything I said, no matter how trivial, would be heard all the more keenly because I was ill.

Georgina's case of typhoid was more aggressive than ours. For a period of fifteen nights, her temperature rose so high that she had to be wrapped in freezing cold sheets, a procedure that caused me a certain envy, since the only time I was ever wrapped in damp sheets, the feeling it gave me was so mysterious that I seemed to be descending into an unknown place.

Though the governess could have helped her, Mother worked day and night, allowing no one else to give us our medicine, or to do anything else at all during her brief absences. The French doctor who cared for us sometimes spent all night at our house, since his own was so far that it would have been impossible to call him in an emergency.

It was on this occasion, once we were out of danger, that Mother voiced her opinion, in front of everyone, that I was the sweetest girl, the one who always smiled, the one who caused her no trouble when I was ill. I felt fondly toward myself, and since I never asked for anything, and liked for the long hours to go by one by one as I drowsed, and would almost have preferred for no one to turn my pillows, or offer to make my bed, I learned early on why certain kinds of people have always so exasperated me when they are ill. Though I might do my utmost for them, I nonetheless pretended not to notice the exaggerated scale of their complaints, since I was convinced that they were exploiting their illness, that they were taking advantage of the circumstances to get attention, to ask for things, to complain and to be ill-humored . . . as if it were necessary to make a fuss, as if a fevered state weren't one of the loveliest feelings, and convalescence weren't enveloped in a vague and fleeting magic.

Since then, I have often thought that very few people deserve, even for only one night, to dwell in the strange world brought on by fever, or in that other world of convalescence, full of siestas and brief dreams that come by surprise, when one is free of haste or useless anxiety to live as others do.

Only once, when I was seriously ill, did my sleeplessness seem too haunted and unfamiliar to face in silence for hours on end. Mother was also ill and had been taken to a clinic, and I felt so alone, so far from everyone, in that night when only I would remain awake, and it seemed so dreadful that she wasn't beside me and knew nothing of my affliction, that for the sake of clinging to something familiar and dear, I gradually heightened the details of her absence and my fear. When my anguish became impossible to bear, I asked Irene to hold my hand, or to run hers over my brow, and though the night was near its end and Irene was very tired, my fear – the morphine, my splitting head, the room full of lamps – made me demand that gesture which, the following morning, would fill me with regret.

When Mother was brought home and came into my room, fragile, half happy, half sad, the new distance we had each traveled made us smile with moistened eyes, and it was all we could do to embrace each other on my bed and cry.

When the typhoid fever waned, they began to feed us, but we were allowed to eat so little that when we were brought our tea and milk with two or three lumps of sugar, we invented the method of removing the sugar and drinking the bitter tea. We placed the little cubes on our pillows, taking care for Mother not to see, and after we drank our tea, we would eat them slowly, making them last a long time; but our pillowcases all had a damp, sticky little circle we couldn't hide.

Once we were strong enough to get out of bed, so much of our hair was falling out that our heads had to be shaved. There is still a photograph of the five of us, dressed identically, arranged in order of height, making up a staircase of smooth, shiny heads. If not for this unseemly detail, it would have been a perfect convalescence.

She came to see us twice. Tall and dressed all in white, she arrived in a sulky she drove herself. Before coming in she took off one glove, then stepped toward the horse to feed it a lump of sugar.

On her second visit, she brought a small parcel she untied slowly with her long, stiff fingers. She gave each of us a necklace and spent an hour on the terrace, gazing at us as if searching for a memory gone astray. When Mother offered her a cup of tea, she accepted immediately, but then didn't take even a sip, and before she left, asked in a slightly mournful voice if she might have a glass of water with some drops of lemon juice. On that occasion, Mother waved when the sulky rounded the bend before the avenue of poplars, and we forgot to ask who she was.

I often saw her pass vaguely alongside other memories, and came close to asking her name and why she didn't come back to visit. Something prevented me, and much later, when I remembered her, I preferred to hold onto the mystery of her sudden appearance in the little sulky, or picture her sitting on the terrace, her big straw hat in her lap.

I also remember that before she left she slowly unraveled, thread by thread, all of the ribbons tied around the gifts, as if she were alone and waiting for something.

Susana and I looked on as Irene, Marta, and Georgina got ready, as Mother took such care to place small orange-blossom wreaths on our sisters' heads, from which white tulle flowed to the floor. As the governess's hands adjusted a fold and Madame Lagrange's straightened a curl, we felt terribly empty, as if we'd suddenly been left alone.

Marta was the least shy of the three, the one who looked best in her First Communion dress. As she approached the altar between the other two, I'm sure she was convinced she was entering one of those marvelous dreams that occupied her childhood, and conferred on her that calm and indifferent air.

Irene, as always, filled us with admiration. She was so tall no one would have believed she was only fourteen, and when she bowed her head after taking communion, she looked so pale that I noticed for the first time – despite having heard it often – how pretty she was; to me, she had always seemed too much as if she were blooming, and in those days I couldn't imagine that beauty might go hand in hand with an air of health.

Georgina's tiny figure was closer to my heart, and when I gazed at her, I briefly satisfied my weakness for anything helpless, anything needing to be watched over and protected.

We left the church and went to the studio of the only photographer in town, a young man who walked about as if continually searching for something. When he turned to look at his camera, he would spin back around quickly on one foot, revealing a pallid face and an almost pink, narrow-lipped mouth that smiled as if he'd caught someone by surprise in an awkward situation. As he positioned my sisters in front of a folding screen, he took their chins between his thumb and forefinger, and after trying ten times to find their most flattering angle, took a small balletic jump back and arranged himself into a sweet and effeminate pose.

That morning in the studio we saw on the table a shoebox shrouded by a kerchief, which, when he noticed our interest, he lifted with great care. Inside, motionless, a white rabbit with pink, cloudy eyes lay dying, so slowly that the photographer kept returning his gaze to the box, taking advantage of any excuse – while he left his clients surrounded by columns and Versailles staircases – to go over on tiptoe and attend to his rabbit's death.

Susana and I stayed beside the box while our sisters tried to hold their pose. When I heard the shutter snap, my gaze drifted instinctively from the rabbit to Georgina's sheer, white figure. I don't know why, but Georgina seemed somehow linked to the large, white rabbit, and I had to make sure that her eyes weren't pink, but blue and gleaming.

As I stroked the rabbit I began to feel afraid, and decided to get closer to Susana and ask if she'd noticed the likeness, but at that moment the photographer covered the box and bid us goodbye, as if wishing to be alone for those silent death throes, in which everything seemed so entirely pleasant and proper.

All afternoon, I tried not to think of what had happened, but when my sisters took off their white dresses, I was convinced I would find no relief until I said it aloud.

I was sure she had come to love us during the two years she spent in our house, but she missed her country more and more by the day, and whenever we asked if she was happy in Argentina, she answered evasively, as if reminiscing, in a voice so remote that we didn't dare to insist, "I have many dead buried in Valencia . . . "

The afternoon before she left, she asked Mother to go to her room, so she could show her what she was taking in her trunks. Mother refused, but when she insisted, she had no choice but to agree. Mother cast an eye over her clothing and other possessions, unmoved, and was about to leave the room when she noticed a small wooden box among the trunks. The maid hurried to open it. It was full of dirt, small mounds of dust like those picked up by the dustpan when a room has been swept.

"I'm taking some dirt from the garden, and a little dust from the rooms."

She had found a way to quietly show us her fondness for Argentina.

I remember the Saturday nights. The entire week's happy routine led up to that day. We knew it was different from all the others and that not even Sunday – free of schoolwork or any kind of activity – brought us close to such a simple night, so filled with joy, so completely ours, as Saturday.

Among the large and small details I retain are the tiny white organdy aprons Mother would wear to serve us tea; the moment – always jubilant – when I would set foot on the first step of the brake; the thick slices of watermelon that Pascual, the driver, would give us; the concrete barn, divided into sections, where two hundred rabbits lived; the horses' shiny, damp necks; the brandied grapes that Mother prepared in big jars (sometimes she made us close our eyes and open our mouths and fed us a huge, strange, alcoholic grape we would savor for a long while); Esthercita's glee when she was bathed; the pride I felt when standing between my father's knees as he drove the horses; my gratitude when Mother said I had always caused the least trouble and was the easiest when I was ill; the rainy afternoons when we had to play inside . . . Nothing, not a single other reminiscence, reawakens those times in me – with such clear truth – and brings me such a perfect sense of them as those Saturday nights.

At dusk on that day, almost throughout the year, we were given a hot bath after playtime. Susana and I were bathed together, one at each end of the big bathtub. At first, Mother's hands gave us light shivers as she soaped our backs. The lit stoves in the bedrooms, the warm towels and nightgowns, all of the details of those nights remain inside me. The distance of the years makes them no less sweet, no less unmistakable.

Once bathed, we all climbed into bed and were given a big glass of hot milk. Then the same comments about the fresh sheets would begin, the same tips for keeping our whole bodies warm, until one of us was brave enough to stick out an arm, and another to prop herself up against her pillow. A few minutes later, our older sisters' voices came to meet ours. That night, the light would stay on a long while, and the doors between our rooms would stay open until we fell asleep.

From our invisible beds the voices came, enveloped in fresh silences; our words acquired a confiding, mysterious tone rarely heard at other times. We knew every Saturday would be the same as the last, but once we lived it, we could conceive of no change, and we approached those nights as if already sensing that from the fleeting comfort they provided would come something deep-rooted and enduring.

Little by little, the words grew further apart, and after a silence more persistent than the others, Irene's voice, a little bit drowsy, would begin to dream up the portion of mystery to which she was most passionately drawn, and tell us of kidnappings and elopements, of someone awaiting her by the row of poplars. Sometimes, Marta would parade before us the list of important people she'd like to be, and the younger three would fall silent, half-asleep, since we didn't yet know the nature of our own dreams. Mother would tiptoe in later than usual and discreetly cover a shoulder or smooth a blanket and then withdraw, turning out all the lights as she went.

Sometimes, I am overcome by nostalgia, the nostalgia caused only by tiny, simple things, by the most unassuming events of all. This is my memory of those Saturday nights, which come back to me on a great wave of gentleness and purity, bringing me the knowledge that my childhood could not have been sweeter.

In the garden, my father had set up a game we called the "run-claff." I have never seen anything like it since. It was made of a thick pole that rose about four meters from the ground, with a square, spinning platform attached horizontally at the top, and four knotted ropes hanging at intervals from its corners. Each hanging on to a rope with both hands so as not to slip, the four of us would set off running. As the platform spun faster and faster, we scarcely grazed the dirt with one foot, until great waves lifted us far off the ground, then lowered us again in a rapid, circular flight.

On one occasion, Irene, Marta, Georgina, and I held on to the ropes as usual and began to run. Once we were in full swing, it suddenly occurred to me that I wouldn't be able to stop or land back on the ground when I pleased. I was terrified to think that, if my sisters refused to stop, I would be forced to keep flying for hours on end.

Later, in schools, on underground trains, and in elevators, I became familiar with a similar kind of distress. I didn't mind staying in the same place for hours on end, but found it essential to know I could leave whenever I liked. If the doors at a play or a concert were closed to prevent people coming in late, I would immediately check to see if they could be opened from inside. Otherwise, I preferred to leave the performance.

Determined to see once and for all how much anxiety I could bear, I tried crying to my sisters that I was tired. But they thought I was joking and wouldn't stop running long enough for me to let go.

A genuine fear drove me to insist that they stop. I rose up in the air in silent, undulating flight, and they refused again. I decided to take my chance to let go of the rope when the next curve came, since I had to do so at the moment when I was highest, to fall far away and prevent my sisters from crashing into the post.

A few seconds went by before I decided to hurl myself down. The four of us were spinning incessantly, almost horizontally around the post. When the upward curve accentuated, I loosened my grip on the rope, heard my sisters scream, and fell onto the path. Though my knees were bleeding and one of my hands felt numb, I got to my feet and told them that I was fine. At least I had banished my fear.

The years go by, distancing me from her birth, from the always fresh joy to which she accustomed me, and from her sudden, untimely death. But even today, her name stirs up everything all at once, and I see how, next to her tiny figure, Mother regains from so far away the expressions that flow, perhaps more powerfully, from her to me.

While Mother was expecting Esthercita, her modesty left us only a half-open window onto the sewing room, and even her silhouette, viewed against all I preserve of my childhood, never looked unusual, never hinted at any swelling beneath all the ribbons and lace.

I do not know whether another child was a source of joy or perhaps of sadness, of fear. Her discretion prevented her usual gestures from betraying a change, and her tenderness was as simple and persuasive as always.

The only sign that Esthercita was on the way was the sudden appearance of a nurse, whose white uniform brought a serenity and orderliness to the hallways that led us to suspect that something unusual was afoot. When she came toward us we looked at her shyly. She was so tall and ugly that I still remember her with a certain amount of compassion.

Could she have been the one to inspire the pity I've always felt for tall, ungainly women, whom I assumed would be always alone? They seemed so awkward when they were sad . . . !

As if they couldn't cry, as if they ought not to cry, as if, for them, everything was more painful. It always saddened me to hear of a tall woman suffering from unrequited love, and, inevitably, without understanding why, I would imagine her shoes, so graceless, so impossible to hide, until my gaze fell on her feet, which represented one of the many things I have always sought to avoid.

The first time we saw the nurse, Mother stayed in bed; she had us called into her room to bid us each farewell, more lovingly than ever, and told us we would spend the day at Madame Lagrange's quinta.

When we came home, the nurse was waiting on the terrace to take us to Mother's room.

My father sat up when he heard us enter. On the pillow, beside Mother's slightly pale face, a hollow betrayed the recent pressure of a head. But we had no time to dwell on this detail. We saw a cradle, with a large pink bow and a new set of drapes. Mother asked us to come closer, and the nurse's hands, nudging us forward, lessened our shyness.

We looked inside, a little ashamed, none of us daring to say the first word.

"Do you know who this is?" Mother asked, in a voice that seemed proud and slightly tearful. "It's your new little sister . . . "

Standing on tiptoe, leaning over the cradle, all of us kissed the small, narrow path of her forehead. Esthercita.

I can't remember which book or comment led me, for a few days, to feign a serious mood, a solemn and pensive attitude. When my sisters called me to play, I answered in a tone of concentration, "I can't. I have too much to think about."

My sisters gathered around, tugging at my dress, laughing and dancing about me, holding hands. Unmoved, determined to continue my brooding, I would wander off and sit alone in a corner of the terrace.

On the third day, when I realized that no one was impressed, I began to tire of my act. When classes were over and it was time to play, I tried to approach my sisters, but they, intent on getting revenge, left me alone.

Prepared not to show a single regret, a single change in my behavior, that afternoon I stayed alone by the terrace, casting sidelong glances as they finished a game of croquet with the governess. My efforts to think about something complicated, to seem absorbed in the deepest of thoughts, were futile; I felt overwhelmingly bored and forlorn.

The next afternoon, to dispel the isolation I'd brought on myself, I went over to them and said, "Shall we play croquet?"

My sisters looked at me but pretended not to notice, until one of them said, "You can't play with us. You have too much to think about." Then they ran off toward the garden.

Half an hour later, when she came into my room, Miss Whiteside found me crying alone on my bed. Without saying a word, she dried my eyes with her handkerchief and smoothed my hair. Then I heard one of my sisters coming. After a few minutes, they were all in my room, chatting away about trivial things, until I forgot my loneliness and joined in the conversation.

When they described the horse's drawn-out dying moments, his body surrounded by hot coals in the stable yard, his whinnies shorter and shorter, further and further apart, his death seemed to acquire the exact shape I would have foreseen, had I imagined it.

The day my father decided to get a new horse – pitying his dapple-gray, now old, and afraid of tiring him out – he didn't imagine that the horse would long for his old routine of meeting him every morning, hearing his voice as he caressed his neck, and crouching almost to the ground so he could mount effortlessly.

The first time no one went to saddle him up, he stayed by the fence, his ears aquiver, watching as the new horse was led by its bridle to the terrace where my father stood. Once he lost sight of the horse and heard only its distant gallop, he let out a plaintive neigh and spent all morning pacing back and forth in the paddock, waiting for something that might explain this unusual abandonment. As if he too had longed for him, when my father returned from his morning ride, he went to see his old horse, to speak his usual words of affection.

But the next morning, the horse's eyes, even more astonished, followed the same scene as the day before. When my father approached to stroke him, he rested his head against his arm more intently than ever, as if to prevent him from

70

leaving on the new horse, then sadly watched my father prepare before he set off at a gallop.

Far from his companions, the dapple-gray soon began to gallop around the paddock in the peculiar way of unsaddled horses. For a few minutes he stood, nervously twitching his ears, until suddenly, as if feeling unstoppable despair at that clatter of hooves, he set off at a gallop toward the wire fence, clearing it with a leap.

There was a faltering, heartrending neigh. When the driver ran toward the horse, he found him outside the paddock, his leg caught in the barbed wire. When he jumped, he had torn his belly open against a post.

Several farmhands carried him straight to the stable. From there, his painful and haunting whinnies reached us. When my father returned, the horse's long death throes had already begun. Surrounded on all sides by hot coals to keep him warm, for hours he lay there, stiff, his eyes fixed on the same point. To see if they could still recognize anyone, my father kneeled on the ground, trying to place himself within reach of those wide and mournful eyes.

Pascual, the driver, watched over him all afternoon and all night. The next morning at dawn, when my father went to the stable, his dapple-gray had already died.

He died of jealousy. That's how I understood it, and that's what I wish to keep on believing forever.

Mother had just dismissed the cook. Irene sat on her bed, with her dresses, toys, and all her worldly possessions piled up by her pillow, weeping softly. She was always the one to drive the servants away. She moved their things around, hid the most important utensils, shouted things at them while hiding behind a door, and made up a thousand arguments so Mother would end up begging them to leave.

But Irene had liked María right from the start, and when she learned that Mother had dismissed her, she went off in search of María and begged her to say when she was leaving, so that they could make their escape together. The cook was touched and said she would leave the next morning; only after forcing her to promise to wake her in time did Irene return to her room. Silently, pretending not to understand the jokes made at her expense, crying tears that went unheard, she set about wrapping up her clothes and books and all of her little things, and when she had made a bundle almost as big as herself, she lay down in bed, since she would have to get up early.

The next morning, the cook left without saying goodbye. When Irene realized she had been deceived, she went sadly back to her room to hang up her clothes, untie her books, and put all her things back in their place.

She wore such a tragic expression that, for the first time, we didn't dare follow her.

I remember how, though there were many of us, when Mother relayed the latest amusing episode to her friends – the new words we repeated, the gestures we copied from the grown-ups – she always listed separately, and in a different tone, the characteristics she noted in each of us.

One of the things on which her affection dwelled – as if she went over those memories often, so as to keep them whole, and remembered them with the same delight I would later take in recalling certain episodes, to try out the memory and shield it from being forgotten – made me feel so helpless, I found it impossible to listen calmly. This happened, without fail, when Mother would reminisce about the details of our baptisms.

Our enthusiasm for children – which occupied hours on end as we played at how we would each dress our own, the names we would like to give them – worsened my discontent, since, almost by accident, I would be transported back to my imaginary baptism, returning to our game in the knowledge that it was too late, that it was impossible to make it happen again. When we performed the ceremony among ourselves, each of us playing a different role, we dressed our dolls in long lace robes, and it never occurred to me that the tender picture of a child in its godmother's arms, with a gown almost touching the floor, might be absent from anyone's life.

One day, as Mother recounted the details of each sister's baptism, I learned that all of them had been baptized a few months after birth, wrapped in their long, white gowns made of lace, except for me. When I learned this – I must have been six – it had no great effect at first. I was a little sorry, but felt resigned and didn't say anything, since Mother explained that when I was a few months old, my father was leading an expedition and she'd promised to wait for his return.

It wasn't until later that I began to feel a bit sorry for myself. Leaning on Mother's memories, I imagined myself at two years old – the age I was baptized – dressed in white, with bows and lace just like the others, but in a short outfit that didn't even cover my knees. Someone took me by the hand as we entered the church, but let me climb the steps to the altar all by myself. I imagined that only then would they have tried to hold me in their arms, and though I tried to convince myself that on that occasion I was just as sweet as other children, I sensed that something was missing, that the scene lacked the same gravity and charm; that though the dress was new, it wasn't a baptism gown, and that I might have kept wearing it on Sundays, rather than having it put away in a trunk like those of my sisters.

But I didn't dare confide my disappointment in anyone. When Mother told the story, I felt wistful, as if I slightly pitied myself. I would have preferred for her not to tell it, or at least never to have known about it myself. I was a little ashamed and afraid of blushing; I had a feeling that someone else would find it just as mortifying as I did that I had to climb the steps to be baptized all by myself. My childhood, I was convinced, had been incomplete; it lacked that joy others found in theirs, and preserved in their memories.

Georgina was the only one who could get her straight off to sleep. Unlike my older sisters, I never had the privilege of lulling Esthercita to sleep, and even if I'd been allowed, I would rarely have been able to savor the chance, since Marta and Georgina were always competing for her.

When Esthercita wouldn't rest, she was usually passed to Georgina, so she could try and lull her to sleep. Georgina had her own "method" and would go into Mother's room, then join us again in the garden a few minutes later with a satisfied air of accomplishment.

One afternoon, we decided to find out why it was that Esthercita fell asleep so quickly with her. We huddled behind the curtains and watched Mother change and get Esthercita ready, until she handed her to Georgina, wrapped up in a white blanket.

Georgina paced back and forth with Esthercita in her arms, then sat down on the huge bed. Esthercita, as always, seemed to pretend to be asleep, closing her eyes briefly then opening them again, her large pupils unglazed by any shadow. That was when Georgina took the chance to apply her method. When Esthercita's hesitant eyelids began to droop, only to open again, Georgina blew gently upon them. She didn't even have to do it twice. Esthercita had already fallen into the deepest slumber.

Ever since we were very small, Susana and I had grown so accustomed to hearing the phrase in English "They aren't pretty, but what lovely hair they've got!" that sometimes we would step in and say it ourselves, without any hint of impudence, when someone came to visit or a friend of Mother's stroked our heads.

For a long time, though, my sisters made fun of our flame-red hair, and once even claimed that we weren't our mother and father's daughters, but had been taken in and adopted by them.

Susana and I gazed at each other and our doubts began to grow. The color of our hair seemed to separate us from the others, whose fair heads would later be just like Mother's. Papa's reddish beard didn't convince us that we were related, since we were persuaded that everything came from the maternal side.

When the jokes became too insistent, we cried in the knowledge that, one day, we would be forced to leave home and say farewell to Mother, Papa, and our sisters. Marta whispered that I would have to work, and would be the black sheep of the family just like in *Little Women*, which we had read with the governess, and to whose characters we used to compare ourselves. For a long time, the dark term *black sheep*, and the conviction that I was adopted, bound me more and more closely to Susana, in anticipation of the day we would have to leave. She, on the other hand, suffered only later for the vibrant shade of her hair, even redder than mine; when she was ten and we came home together from school, she would sometimes pause at a shop window and cry disconsolately, since her blazing hair was reflected so violently in the glass that she could foresee no change that might lessen its intensity.

Sometime later, when I met my maternal grandmother, I heard her say as she stroked my head with a nostalgic look, "Her hair is as lovely as mine when I was young." Overjoyed and triumphant, I went in search of my sister and told her, "Grandmother says her hair was just like mine. We aren't adopted!"

Susana gazed at my hair as if her happiness had depended upon it entirely.

Once, we requested a cook from Buenos Aires and were sent a specimen whose unkempt and bounteous girth housed a fabulous good humor – the physical and moral requisites of an excellent cook. She had been with us just a few days when we discovered her contagious pride, which even today leads us to say, whenever we think of her, "She was cook to the King of Spain."

I don't know if her references bore witness to this claim, but I do know she dreamed up dishes so sublime that they are still remembered in my house. A little too far off now, I can only recall their presentation, the flair with which she placed a green beside a yellow, the spectacular height of some of her desserts, the transparency and proportions of her jellies. Of the recipes themselves, all that survives is the dulce de leche, the corn cakes, and the empanadas she learned to make on arriving in Mendoza, where she stayed four years.

One afternoon, she felt unwell and went to see the doctor in town. Though the diagnosis did nothing to diminish her good humor, she had to have surgery.

She was operated on immediately at the hospital, and, two weeks later, the storied dishes enjoyed by Spanish grandees began to process through our house again.

Both her conduct with the workers and gardeners, and her proximity to the age of fifty placed her beyond suspicion;

nonetheless, soon after she was back in the kitchen, the grown-ups noticed that her belly looked unusual, as if a baby were growing inside it.

When she finally found it impossible to keep quiet, we learned from Mother that she had asked her to palpate her belly, and since there was no explanation for the protuber-ance, which continued to swell, they decided to call the doctor.

After much insistence, she let them reopen the wound, but since she was determined to see for herself what it was hiding, she would only consent to a local anesthetic.

To Josefa's stupefaction and much to the fright of the doctor performing the surgery, at the first slice of the scal-pel, a pair of long, narrow scissors emerged, the kind used to trim bandages. Luckily for the doctor, Josefa was tied to the operating table when he tried to slip the scissors into his apron pocket; when she realized she couldn't sit up to hurl curses, she insulted him under her breath, then insisted on asking in a wry and mocking voice if he hadn't also forgotten his gloves or his white coat, until the exasperated doctor forced her to inhale a strong dose of ether so he could sew up the wound.

When she came round, only the nurse and medical student on duty reaped her fury; but though he evaded it, just a few months later, the doctor had to slip away to another town, since the quips in the local newspaper about surgical implements gone astray had frightened off all his patients.

Josefa, on the other hand, became so popular that it wasn't long before she was spoiled. Each time anyone came to our house, no matter how hard we tried to prevent it, she used any excuse to tell the story about the scissors, until they became a true obsession.

One night, she exaggerated their size so much, recalling them in such exuberant detail and ascribing herself such a magnificent, almost villainous role, that she had to be dismissed. I am sure that when she tells the story now in Spain, she even claims the capricious doctor used gardening implements.

Sometimes, Susana and I would ask each other, "What's the most tragic thing of all? Something that has nothing to do with family, or anyone leaving or dying? The most tragic thing for everyone, that has nothing to do with people?"

Susana would look deep in thought, then parade an army of dead animals, floods, a tree struck by lightning before our eyes. We thought of many things. Those that occurred to me were simpler. I imagined baby birds lying on the ground, cows dead and abandoned in the road, an eagle snatching away a lamb, a snake coiled around a horse, tightening its embrace until it choked.

I always associated tragedy with horses. They seemed to me so decent, so resigned, so silent. When I wanted to imagine an animal in great pain, I never thought of dogs or cats, cows or rabbits. I always pictured a horse.

One night, when we had talked a great deal, I went to bed thinking of my father's dapple-gray, who would crouch down to the ground so he could mount effortlessly. Someone had mentioned a book whose protagonist sinks into a swamp and cannot be saved, where the last thing to be seen is a hand waving, leaflike, over the mud. I thought immediately of a horse, a white horse, gradually sinking into that shifting, viscous mire until only its head could be seen, its desperate mouth, its immense muzzle and sorrowful eyes, filling with stubborn, sticky wet mud.

When Susana asked me again, "What's the most tragic thing of all?" I replied, gazing at her as if delivering terrible news, "A white horse, sinking into a swamp."

Her fingers trembled gently beside the recently opened letter, but her loyalty allowed her no delay, no ideal moment to tell us of her departure.

"I have had news from England. My sister has died. Her children cannot be left alone."

Mother embraced her silently, while we sought an excuse to leave, since we knew our sorrow was so clumsy and inept that we'd be unable to step forward and utter a word. We sensed the agony that was to come, but couldn't trace it to a single day or night while we still had her small, gray figure beside us. We had to arrive at her absence, the moment after her departure, to be able to give shape to our woe.

By dinnertime, speech came with more ease.

"I'll write often," she told us, her sweetness scarcely shaken by a sorrowful murmur.

But that night, we laughed as much as any other. We spoke of her arrival in London, the moment she would alight from the boat to throw herself into her younger sister's arms. We rehearsed the scene, one of us standing at each end of the salon. On a given signal, we would let out a cry and race toward the sister coming to meet us, squeezing each other in a frenzy surpassing all affection, which in the end caused us to roll about on the floor. The tiny governess watched us from her armchair. It seemed as if she were afraid, or as if the curve of her cheek, already tired, were awaiting a tear.

Eight days later, she fastened her suitcases. Mother said goodbye in her room since it was time to feed Esthercita, and as she ushered us onto the terrace, a few tears fell onto her naked breast.

On the terrace, I was the first to say goodbye, since I suspected I wouldn't be able to watch her leave from up close, within reach, and as the embraces came, one after another, with a fondness that thwarted all intentions to stay calm, I slipped discreetly away to my room.

When the last cries reached me from the staircase, I began to sob as never before, and went to the window to catch a glimpse of her for the last time. The brake was already rounding the bend in the drive. Miss Whiteside was sitting up straight, looking toward the house, hat slightly tipped to one side, her hands in her lap.

When we saw her standing at the gate, her baby in her arms, we assumed she was a beggar, though she had an air of desperation about her, as if she were in trouble, rather than the stiff resignation of those who are begging for alms. When the maid went to speak to her, we noticed that after pointing toward the outer edge of the quinta, she gestured and shook the child as if referring to him.

Rosa went to find Mother while we went down to the garden.

"Her little boy is very ill," Rosa explained. "She says the only thing that will cure him is warm cow dung, and she asked permission to go into the corral."

Mother agreed immediately, and though she tried to keep us back, we followed close behind the woman, who dashed toward the corral, muttering to herself and clasping her motionless child in her arms.

When she reached the paddock where the cows were grazing, she slipped through the wire fence, approached the heaps of dung with resolve and, without hesitation, began touching them one by one, until she could tell that none of them were warm enough. Sitting on a pile of logs, eyes wide and imploring, she gazed at the cows, who went on chewing indifferently. Each time a tail swished the woman would tremble, and her face split by rough furrows was calmed, as if some relief or hope for a moment had sweetened it, until she sank again into rocking her child in her arms, which failed to revive him.

After a long wait, she suddenly dashed to the middle of the corral. A faint steam was rising from a pile of dung. A cow watched us with its round and drowsy eyes.

We huddled together fearfully. A flash of relief again crossed the woman's face, but this time paused long enough to calm her mouth pursed in anguish and her fiercely darting eyes.

We saw her undress the child, who didn't even cry. We saw his tiny body, without any lovely curves, completely naked, behind the still and indifferent cow.

She laid him on the ground on his belly, held him down hard with one hand so he couldn't move, and, kneeling by his side, plunged the other into the steaming dung several times, without any sign of disgust, with no mind for anything except the life of her son. The boy lay calm on the ground. Her hand came and went from the dung to his body, until it had shaped an enormous cross on his tiny back.

There was something wild, something furious in her eyes and movements. Once there was no longer any space to fill, she covered the boy with her shawl and left him a long while on the ground. The child didn't move. The woman waited. When the cross she had drawn on his back grew cold, she lifted him carefully, wrapped him up in his rags, and, slipping between the cows, left through the last cattle gate, not seeing us, staring right through us, as if she had now accomplished the miracle of her tenderness and her fear.

Five heads together. A cool breeze on the back of our necks. Five heads together; one dark, two fair, two red. A glacial air constantly at the back of our necks, and below, the blanket – a still strip of shadow slicing the cart horizontally in two – allowing just the occasional glimpse of a yellow stripe on the jaguar skin covering our legs.

Our hands hidden under the blanket, we entertained ourselves by guessing at whose we were squeezing. Pascual's silhouette, unchanging in the driver's seat, moved imperceptibly when the horses slackened their pace. In some places, the wheels carved deep, wet grooves that closed up again immediately. The horses, covered in foam, struggled through the mud, and the cart, swaying from one side to another, brought our heads close together, then separated them again gently as it regained its balance.

All of us recognized Marta's hands as soon as we touched them. Though she had given up the habit of picking at her skin, where it blossomed at her fingertips and on the palm of her hand, her touch reminded us of the rough surface of unsanded wood.

Once, when I brushed against her peeling hand, I declared instinctively that it was hers.

"I'm not playing anymore. You can tell it's me right away," I heard her grumble as she withdrew her hand from mine. Irene hurried to grasp at it in the darkness and to ask in a forced tone, as if wanting to ease Marta's disappointment, since she thought we found her hands so ugly, "Whose is this one?"

When I held Marta's hand in mine once again, I exclaimed, "Whose can it be?"

Our hands fluttered beneath the blanket in the gloom. When we drew near the town, a lamp suddenly lit the cluster of our five heads. For a moment I saw that Marta, with a sad smile, was willing the pretense to go on.

"When you grow up and get married, girls, you'll have to kill hens to make stew for your husbands."

When the gardener told us this, I paid little attention, but still went to my room – since I suspected he was on his way to the henhouse for a chicken to slaughter – while he went off whistling, unconcerned, as if the hen's neck, its incessant flapping then sudden silence, caused him no fear or disgust at all. But one afternoon a while before Christmas, when a turkey was brought to the house to be fattened up, I began to feel squeamish.

What if I married someone without a cook, and he liked to eat chicken once in a while?

I remembered the air of alarm of a cook who burst into the dining room shrieking that the turkey she'd just put in the oven had let out a final gobble, most likely stuck in its throat when its neck had been wrung, and I began to imagine the details of its slaughter. I felt the hen's soft, gritty, repulsive neck, covered in little red spots, as it twisted in all directions. I pictured myself gripping its body between my knees, trying to pull back its head, but the neck stretched like elastic, and when I stopped pulling, the head snapped sharply back into place. Convinced I would miss the head, that I would get the precise spot wrong, at other times I imagined the still-live chicken writhing beside me; my hands and my apron were soaked with a chilling stain, gruesome and thick.

The only thing I couldn't imagine was the first motion. How to grab hold of it. Where to squeeze in order to choke it. How to break its neck. Even if I used an axe, I would have to hold it in one hand while dealing a blow with the other. Then the horror of it would upset me so much that when I struck with the axe, I would split the head in two, or, severing only the crest, spot one of my fingers some distance away, unrecognizable, oozing blood on the table.

Then I assumed that the hen would end up only half-dead, the head dangling off the table, looking up at itself from below, and I felt the same fear as if a strange hand had tried to open my bedroom window, or the fear that made me shudder in the darkness when, without any warning, Irene reached out hers.

For a long time, I was determined never to marry.

I hear notes coming from the piano. The house fills with packages. We have not seen Mother or Miss Whiteside all afternoon.
We wander to and fro. We go out into the garden. We look at
the clock. When will the time come to let down our curls, to
put on our new dresses?

Though we dine with our parents that night, and with Miss
Whiteside, it seems as if dinner will never end.

I hear notes coming from the piano. The doors to the
salon, which were closed all day, are flung wide open. Behind
us, the servants gather timidly by the window. We line up
and approach the spot suddenly lit by the distinct flickering
of colored candles, then read our names on a parcel. Mother
plays a march, ushering us to and from the tree. My sisters'
faces – happy triangles briefly glimpsed through a gap in the
branches – draw near the long threads of stars that hide in the
bushiest part of the tree. The gold and silver ornaments, the
luminous, fragile baubles, suddenly cast tiny, fleeting glints on
a cheek, on a fair head. When my father approaches the tree
to start passing out the gifts, our eyes begin their descent to
its snowy base, where something more lasting awaits.

We look for the right place to pile up the big, colored parcels. Then we open them hurriedly and read the name on the
gift. Each one implies a kiss, and for half an hour, the heads
of Mother, my father, and Miss Whiteside, and our own tilt

to imprint on a cheek a gesture which, that night, takes on a more pronounced and repeated tenderness.

The candles, now defeated, start leaning to one side. The tree darkens, with its open, laden branches. On the flounces of cotton wrapped around the trunk, a green, red, or yellow teardrop tells of the end of that humming, already distant night.

Before the tree is swallowed by shadows, we drink champagne by the last of the swaying lights. In the dimness, my parents' hands reach toward a small candle leaning too far to one side at the top of the tree. Neither the late hour nor the champagne can halt our impatience, and at midnight, we withdraw to our rooms laden with gifts, eager to compare them and possess them peacefully in the bedrooms' low light.

This was how we would spend Christmas Eve. If my childhood hadn't known those huge parcels, that late, keen ritual, that poignant and slightly dreamlike midnight . . .

In the morning, a big baby doll with fluttering eyes, a game of patience, or the tick-tock of a watch repeated the certainty of that night, which, despite its perfection, I loved to contemplate even more from the next day, in the tangible truth of the gifts that were proof of its fleeting, mysterious, tender reality.

Whenever Mother scolded her, the answer was always the same.

"What am I to do, Señora? I can't disguise it."

She was Eduardito's nanny, and her twenty-five years, a little muted, seemed even more serious due to the shadow of hair on her upper lip.

When we heard her say, for no particular reason, when it was neither here nor there, "I can't disguise it," we couldn't contain our laughter, until one morning, somewhat ill-tempered, Mother explained to her the meaning of the word *disguise*, and added, "If you neglect the baby, it isn't a question of not being able to disguise it. You simply aren't doing your job, because you either don't know how or don't want to."

"Yes, Señora," she answered, but at the first reprimand her reply was the same. Since she was an excellent nanny and loved Eduardito very much, Mother decided to ignore her inevitable response.

One night, when I was crying, she came over to me and said, "You needn't stop crying just because I can see you, child. You don't ever need to disguise it. I feel like crying, too." And she began to cry along with me, until both of us burst out laughing.

By the time I was five, I was used to the mountains' remote and solemn presence, but this landscape did nothing to stir me in any way. People and things gave me the whole tiny world I needed, to be colored in with my favorite words and gestures.

In each faraway scene, leaning against a poplar, shading her eyes with a hand the better to watch us, Miss Whiteside appears, restored to our side, and takes her place, silent and tender, between the two most distant events of my childhood.

Each event is imbued with the same tearful quality. The first has a name – one it kept for such a brief time – the birth of Esthercita. The second, which belonged to Miss Whiteside herself, promising tears that were hers alone, was her departure.

My father had summoned her for a year, but she remained with us for six. The five of us lived for that whole time under her watch, seeing her in her daily sweetness, never knowing – due to her reticence – if in her weariness she ever felt lonely, or if sorrow kept her in her room.

Six years in a strange house, with never a hint of bitterness, never saying a single harsh word, or even having to stifle one. Perfect manners? Excessive affection? Even in love, one slams a door, hears another close it with too much force. While we lived in Mendoza, we never heard a single harsh word. Mother's influence? Perhaps an early conviction that it would be useless? Perhaps her sweetness wouldn't have endured had she been alone or displeased, yet it remains, floating above those six years, and no explanation could lessen its happy truth, and the now distant knowledge that she was so perfect that she needed no kind of finishing touch at all.

Those same poplars that so many times sliced through our view of her now framed her, as she departed, in small, narrow, vertical snapshots, now in profile, now in shadow, as her gloved young English lady's hand failed to conceal a tear.

This is why, as I remember her while perhaps she writes us a letter, still loving us, from the Isle of Man or some remote English village, I must summon her image so that her smile, accustomed to the memory, might pause once again in our own, if she should ever happen to read her name in this book.

"Did you hear that?"

I sat up in bed and tried to make out Susana's face through the gloom, since I suspected she didn't want to admit her fear.

For a moment we remained stiff, and the strange whispering that seemed to be coming from the next room, which had belonged to the governess, was not repeated. The mysterious whispering – a sentence meditated in her now distant affection? – perhaps came from a piece of furniture, a door slightly ajar, a bat that had slipped in during the day.

I stayed awake a long while, to trace the mysterious sound in case we heard it again. It wasn't the noise itself that most terrified me, but my inability to explain it, to know where it was coming from.

At breakfast time, after mentioning our useless fear, Susana told me, "I don't want you to ask me whether I heard anything. I'd rather you said, 'A window just opened, and someone's walking in the next room.' But don't say, 'Did you hear that?' because last night I didn't hear anything until a long time after you asked me, and I don't know if it was the same noise."

For this very reason, once we were in Buenos Aires, when Mother would ask me from her bedroom, "Did you hear that?" I would be gripped by the same fear, since I would immediately become obsessed, and by wondering what might have frightened her, would end up constructing a fear identical to hers, though it had no cause. I was sure that if she had said, "Someone is breaking a lock, or walking through the garden," I would have heard, like Susana, exactly what she described, and not an imaginary, mysterious sound.

Later, whenever I wanted to express a fear, I would begin without any preamble, and when asked whether I'd heard anything unusual, would answer straightaway that I had, since nothing seemed so terrible as suddenly finding oneself alone with a strange noise, one of those noises that strike only once, that pierce through the night, unaccustomed, that cannot be identified, since they almost always stem from other, undefined fears.

For Susana and me, who weren't more than ten, his death did not consist of a day that abruptly ended, split from the night by grief.

We were each oblivious to the details that might have helped us foresee it; from the afternoon he suddenly took ill, we never saw him again, since Mother was the only one to stay by his side.

One morning, very early, we were sent to our French teacher's house. This occurrence, which before had brought us the joy of Esthercita's birth, led us to believe that something was afoot whose mystery we couldn't possibly guess at – behind the closed doors, in the driver's fearful eyes, in the way the horses rushed us away from the house.

When we returned at dusk, as he was carried to the cemetery, the whole town trailing behind him, Mother came into our room.

"I have something to tell you," she murmured, gazing at us from a new and desperate place, her chin trembling in a way so different from the quiver that foretold a smile. "Papa has died." And she fell silent, overcome with an anguish that clouded her eyes.

Susana smiled to herself. I looked out of the window. It was as if I were seeing it for the first time, just as I later realized that everyone, when confronting terrible news, fixes on an object – the first they can find – and never forgets it. The pale-curtained window sustained me, my eyes took in all its details: the way the ruffles fell, the neat little path of the seams, the ties holding the curtains open. My father's death shivered, in all its fullness, against the window.

Mother cried, and we drew near so we could touch her. We didn't know what to do or say. We didn't even ask if he had already been taken away. In fact, we wouldn't have known how to approach him. We never saw him lying down, nor can I remember him without a collar, in shirtsleeves, or in a *robe de chambre* except on Sundays, when he entertained himself by tending the garden.

I do not know how Susana and the others felt on his death. When Mother left the room, the news suddenly seemed to expand, as if the sound of the door had risen in a final, mournful groan. I felt a lump in my throat. I wanted to cry. A ten-year-old will cry for any reason, but I wanted to cry sweetly, so that my tears would be different, unlike any others. I wanted to cry on purpose, to remember every tender moment, so that my tears might last longer than other times. But there was no need. My unconscious memory was crowded with daily scenes, gestures suddenly imbued with lasting meaning, since the person who'd inhabited them was dead. I saw the long hallway that opened into all of the bedrooms, his empty study with no light under the door . . . on the globe, Norway drifted away forever. Closer by, the bedroom, with the cradle drawn near the big bed. Then I remembered his riding crop hanging from its hook.

I began to cry. I cried for hours, while Susana sat very seriously, unable to say a word, as if the pain had settled quietly into her enormous eyes.

For the next few days, our mother's dark silhouette, the silent atmosphere, the preparations to go back to Buenos Aires, our interrupted studies, and our free time prevented me from dwelling on his death. Only several months later, when I read a report of a speech in one of the newspapers Mother kept, did I begin to see it more clearly as painful and final. Among all the tributes paid to him, I picked out a phrase that was free of any rhetorical pretension, whose evocation of his memory was natural and precise. "He was so strong, he fell like an oak; only reeds can stand erect again after a storm."

Some years later, I began to feel proud of his name, but all new respect instilled by his memory came through Mother, and though I still felt he was distant and unknown, he was made near again, sweet and familiar, even in her most daily gestures.

When I see his portrait, I think of how I don't know him; I think of how he doesn't know me.

His death changed the course of our lives.

Bent over the last trunks, her eyes sore from crying so much, Mother secured a lock, packed some forgotten item. We watched her comings and goings, waiting for her to be busy long enough to give us a chance to slip away into the garden. When we saw her pause at the table, a thick sheaf of papers in her hand, we exchanged the sign we had agreed upon, and met moments later on the avenue of poplars at the edge of the quinta.

"Let's start by the gate," Irene announced.

The shadows of the tree trunks scarcely allowed our own, much smaller and thinner, to lie at wide intervals across the ground.

Once at the gate, we let Irene wander a few meters away from us. Marta went after her, followed by Georgina, Susana, and me, all of us terrified by the darkness, by the strange figures the moon conjured between the trees' branches.

It was the last night we were to spend in Mendoza. We had each felt a desire, a tender longing, to say farewell, one by one, to the trees we knew so well and would no longer see.

Irene's silhouette grew smaller beside the huge trunks and her head drew near them just for a moment. A little behind her, we did the same: we kissed the rough bark of a branch, the sweet, fresh dew on a leaf that grazed our face. Sometimes we had to stand on tiptoes to reach a high branch. Sometimes we tried to prevent a trunk with coarse bark from hurting our lips.

101

When we went back to the house, none of us dared to speak. We headed in silence up to our rooms.

Once I was in bed, it seemed our goodbyes should have lasted longer, and from that night on, I became familiar with the strange voluptuousness of farewells. When I imagined myself on the eve of a long absence, I scanned the atmosphere in the utmost detail – the tender gestures, the words I would utter if it was one day my turn to leave. I suspected that nothing else could equal the tone of slowly murmured sorrow that surrounds farewells, and by lengthening them indefinitely, I forced them to return so that they would begin again, in the bend in a train's journey that suddenly offers up the same window, or the turn of a boat that brings back the person at the prow; and when I imagined bidding anyone goodbye, I took care for the scenes to repeat themselves, for the embraces to never end, for a special, unforeseen moment to always occur, when a mouth is recovered or a goodbye spoken in a tone already accustomed to sorrow.

How can it be, I used to wonder, that anyone should avoid that thrill so as not to face the grief that strikes, by day or by night, when things take on greater depth, when one feels more goodness, more solitude . . . ?

As I kissed the trees in Mendoza I was already close to this fervor that farewells have always brought out in me. But when we went to bed that night, not saying a word to each other, we had no idea that fifteen years later we would have to repeat the same routine with the old trees on Calle Tronador.

We had arrived in Mendoza, the five of us, dressed in our white sailor's outfits. We set out for Buenos Aires dressed in mourning. Between our departure and our return by train: Esthercita's birth and my father's death. One new name, the other now pronounced in memory, in that faltering voice used to speak at first of those no longer living, until habit gradually places their names in trivial conversations, in minor scenes, which come to life only because behind them stir the dead.

Leaning on our elbows out of the windows, we followed the little clumps of grass that huddled by the other tracks; at the occasional bend, we recovered our view of the hazy silhouette of the mountains.

"There they are again!" one of us would cry. At that moment, they existed for us alone with the special tenderness of a farewell, when one scans a ship's deck at length to collect for a second, just one more, the familiar image erased by distance.

The mountains had never interested me. They loomed in the window then slipped away, but I didn't notice. Perhaps I would have been drawn to them if a slice of shadow had outlined a face in their crags, if it had endowed them with painful meaning, or if it weren't so clear that they were enough for themselves. But for the six years we lived in Mendoza, I never glimpsed in them what always most drew me to things, that sudden sense they gave of feeling alone, the need for them to change in appearance, for them to know humility and helplessness.

Irene was flipping through a magazine. Her black gauze dress added no years, did nothing to lessen her girlish appearance. Marta and Georgina were playing with Esthercita. Meanwhile, Susana and I had a window to ourselves and had long conversations, counted the telegraph poles, or watched a horse crossing the road, while Eduardito dozed on our mother's lap.

After a few hours, two or three heads began to droop by the misted windowpane. Mother thought it a good idea to have an early dinner. A little while later, we followed her all in a row, Eduardito clinging to her hand, and Esthercita in Marta's arms.

A little sad, a little preoccupied, tripping along the narrow aisle in a line, we stepped fearfully from one car to the next – glimpsing the earth flash by at our feet for just an instant, always the same, always different – thrust forward by the train's jolts, until we reached the dining car.

Outside, the night – the sorrow of trains hurtling into other, denser, less familiar shadows – grasped at the windowpanes while I passed the time gazing at my sisters reflected in them.

One train leaves, another returns. Our childhood remained frozen outside the station of a small town.

Four days had passed since we had reached the house on Calle Tronador. We didn't yet fully know where the trees cast their shadows at different hours, but as we sifted through our memories of the early years, little by little we began to recover the clump of Guadua bamboo, the privet hedges, and the flower beds that felt only the lack of some boxwood to be complete.

The elderly neighbors had seen us in our little row, just a few years old, and when they watched our fair-haired procession, now grown and increased in number, they repeated our names as if needing only to recognize them to place us in some distant vision. Doña Nastasia's eyes filled with tears. She was ninety, and we would see her reach a hundred and more, always upright, clinging like bindweed to the walls of the old house that her grandchildren were always conspiring to wrest away from her.

That night, the doctor was called. All afternoon, we had passed the time by making small baskets of flowers for Esthercita to carry as she strolled through the trees. But when the time came to lull her to sleep, we noticed she couldn't get comfortable, and that her brow was clammier than usual.

When the doctor came, we had already gone to bed. From there we heard Mother's voice and the creak of the old doors, tired of moving. We sensed a furtive air in everything happening on the other side.

After a while, we heard a moan. It sounded nothing like Esthercita's voice, her usual way of crying or asking for something. Her sweetness was so drowsy, so delicate, that we only ever heard her light steps through the house, or glimpsed, against the window, a ringlet burning beneath the sun.

In the bedroom adjacent to the one I shared with Susana, Marta's cross voice, compelled by her affection, was growing impatient.

"I must see what's going on. I have to do something."

Susana and I joined the others. In our nightgowns, stiff with cold, we all followed her to Mother's bedroom. At the door we heard the murmur of voices; soon after, a hollow, dismal silence. The clink of a spoon raised a question, and suddenly we heard a moan that sounded like a cry already spent before it had even risen to her lips.

I thought of her mouth, too soft, too tender to house such anguish, and of the small, very pale groove beneath her nose. Whenever I heard anyone say that a child "looked like a doll," I was convinced that Esthercita was the only one who, with her added, sweet liveliness, truly resembled the babies in big toy shops. Above her blue eyes, her narrow, sharply defined eyebrows edged her forehead with a brief and serious little curve, and her long lashes grew separately, as if someone had carefully placed them there one by one. Before dropping off to sleep, as she settled her head in our laps, she would open and close her eyes, and her eyelids fluttered rhythmically like those of big dolls that lower their waxy lids when you tip them back.

Mother came when she heard the patter of our bare feet. She seemed afraid, and wouldn't look us in the eye.

"Esthercita is very ill. She's having convulsions and there's nothing I can do. Go back to bed. The doctor will stay with me. I don't want you to hear, it's too terrible . . . "

Her flat voice sounded foreign, emptied of tenderness. We knew, though, that pain had taken over her whole body, her throat and her limp hands, in which our affection could place nothing but a brief question.

"Is she dying?" A bitter voice unconsciously spoke, as if scarcely concerned, the fear we all shared.

Mother tried to shield us from the truth.

"Good God, don't say such a thing! Go back to bed. I'll call you if there's any need."

The closed door placed a new world before our eyes. We had never come up against the sorrow of a closed door, and sensed that, on the other side, a tiny death would have the same way of opening windows, moistening eyes, making lips turn cold.

In the early hours, the house fell silent. Somebody bolted a door, as if it mattered. Mother came in to cry with us.

When I saw her all dressed up in her tiny coffin, she looked more than ever like one of those big baby dolls lying in a box.

I couldn't cry like the others, or approach and look at her closely. I was afraid of smiling. I understood in that moment that crying was the only way to show my pain. But my eyes were dry. I would have given anything for a tear to roll down my cheek, for the others to see it. Afraid I was going to smile, I went to my room. The light from the chandeliers drew a long stripe on the hall floor.

When they closed the small casket, we heard a groan. I thought it might have been the last she'd exhaled the night before, that only now was echoing through the room. But it was Mother.

Then I saw the grim carriage, so distant from all that she was, which only made the anguish of letting her go alone, with her four sweet years, inside her little white casket, more immense. I thought it would have been gentler and more tender to bury her in the garden beside a big tree, or that at least a woman should go with her, to lower her into the ground with more tenderness.

When the carriage turned at the corner of Calle Tronador, I finally felt my throat harden, until I choked on my tears.

That was how I saw my first death. Her death. Her tiny death.

For two years, she was my best friend, but although we agreed on many things, her taste for anything tinged with sorrow was a constant cause of flashes of ill humor.

I was fond of bustling streets where the neighbors chattered, where we ran races with the boys and rang the doorbells, or played tricks on pedestrians with bunches of flowers on a piece of string, or parcels containing only a bit of rubble. She, on the other hand, liked to sit down on a pile of paving stones in a barren plot with old trees silhouetted against the sky, waiting in silence for the brief and flickering dusk.

When we asked if we would see her the next afternoon, she would object falteringly that she couldn't possibly know what kind of mood she was going to be in. My impatience could not conceive of anyone able to wake in the morning and foresee a bad mood, sorrow, or fatigue, and I would go off convinced it was hopeless to rely on her for anything. At other times, my annoyance drove me to leave her alone, but a while later Susana would discreetly go looking for her, so that she wouldn't think we were feeling bitter.

When we played at visiting houses or fancy dress, she always selected the most pathetic attire. Swathed in tulle, she would swoon to the ground and claim to be a dead bride, then vanish for a few minutes and reappear all dressed in black, her head veiled in crepe, and sit silently with the air of a widow resigned to her fate.

One afternoon, when her melancholy was trying my patience more than ever, I said something mean to her. She pretended not to notice. Half an hour later, as we sat by the side of the street, she looked up at the sky full of dark storm clouds. I thought of the downside of bad weather for Susana and me, since when it rained we weren't allowed to go into the street or play in the garden.

She lifted her huge eyes that seemed to tell so much truth, and said, "If only it would rain tomorrow! Then I can be sad."

Six months after we arrived in Buenos Aires, Mother decided to take on a governess before sending us to school.

One afternoon, a woman dressed in mourning gathered us together in the drawing room. We were very serious and shy, and on her request recited the rivers of Russia, the borders of Spain, the characteristics of Eskimos, the Pythagorean theorem, and the worst habits of domestic animals. Though she seemed satisfied, the governess said condescendingly, "Very well. But you've clearly had foreign teachers. I'm sure you know nothing about our country."

We tried to object with a list of national heroes: San Martín, Belgrano, Moreno, but she interrupted.

"When I say you know nothing, I mean of our language. You lack a thorough understanding of it. I will teach you. To learn Spanish, not only is it essential to know the proverbs, but also to put them into practice. This is my own theory, since I believe proverbs are the foundation of language. Do you know any Spanish proverbs?"

Irene mumbled something about "Where there's smoke . . . " but Señora López annihilated her with the gleam from her spectacles, which looked thick enough to be made for two.

"Let's see," she declared enthusiastically. "You, Marta, go over to the piano and try to move it."

Marta rose reluctantly and leaned against the piano. She never made any effort in vain.

"Can't you manage? Is it very heavy? Let me see, dear, you try and do it," she ordered Georgina, maintaining her air of concentration. Georgina approached the piano shyly.

"You can't manage either? Good. All five of you, please try and move it together."

Pressing against one side of the piano, making a tremendous effort, we managed to push it a few centimeters.

"Excellent!" the teacher exclaimed. "This, in the language of proverbs, illustrates how 'Unity makes for strength.' Marta couldn't move the piano. Nor could Georgina. But all five of you together were successful. Very good. Let's move on to something else."

"We must put it back where it was," Irene objected before Marta's irascible gaze and the indifference of the governess, who was already exploring other practical experiments.

"I want you, little girl, to put all the vases in the drawing room on this table," she ordered Irene, who, thinking the governess required of her an effort as great as the last, gathered most of the vases into her arms. As she approached the table, convinced she had won the game, two of them slipped and were smashed to smithereens on the floor.

"Very good!" Señora López exclaimed again before our astonished eyes. "Had she made two trips, she wouldn't have broken a single vase. The meaning of this, remember it well, is 'Don't bite off more than you can chew.' Will you be so kind as to write that down in your notebooks?"

We quickly jotted it down and assumed we would be let out, since four o'clock had come and it was time for tea. But the governess vanished from the room, and on her return began hurriedly to dictate page after page. It was already six by the time she rose, seeming very pleased. We gaped at her as if she represented only the absence of food.

"You've an appetite, haven't you? I know that tea has been delayed on my account, but I'm doing it for your own good. Before I go, do me the favor of noting down, 'Better late than never.'"

When Mother learned of the moving of the piano, the smashing of the vases, and the timing of our tea, she showed little enthusiasm for the governess's pedagogical methods. Señora López wasn't remotely surprised at her dismissal and bid us all goodbye with the utmost kindness, but before taking her leave, she jangled the ten pesos Mother had given her, and said cheerfully, "A bird in the hand is worth two in the bush."

When we arrived at Tronador, I discovered them right away. After that, on my trips back and forth from the kitchen or the bathroom, it was impossible not to see them every day. They were the only three conspicuous red tiles in the old courtyard. I don't know how they weathered the passage of time, how they didn't fade in the sun.

I remember that, whenever I had to cross the courtyard as night was falling, fearful of all the shadows waiting to ambush me, keeping watch from afar on the great fig tree at the back of the garden which I always imagined was full of men, I could never resist – whether I was in a good or bad mood – taking the little step that connected the first two tiles, and the long step that scarcely allowed me to touch the last.

I don't know why or how I began this routine that later would come to plague me. I think one day, on seeing them, I stepped on two of the tiles. Soon it seemed that the third was also waiting for me, and I grazed it indifferently, not suspecting an urgent game would result from that mysterious, casual deference, which in the event of any trouble, any sorrow, would be impossible to leave aside.

The three tiles anguished and wearied me. Once, I decided to pretend not to notice them, and, treading lightly, crossed the courtyard in a straight line. But as I walked away I felt that the tiles were waiting for me and I had to go back and cross them twice, as if I had cheated them out of something, as if I had slighted them, or broken a promise.

When Esthercita died, I still remember today, I went to the kitchen to pour some coffee. The three tiles came to greet me through my tears, but I feared the short step and the long leap might seem like a pirouette, a game inappropriate for the circumstance. I looked back to make sure that no one could see me, and completed the little jump with tears in my eyes.

Once I had given myself over for good to this custom, the three tiles continued to wield their influence. Even after I turned twenty this troublesome, sometimes vexing habit pursued me. I wanted to forget all about that weakness and fear. But it was impossible. Something forced me to retrace my steps.

Later, when we left the old house, when we bid the ancient trees, the cold, slender railings, and the cracked courtyards farewell, I gazed at the three tiles.

I took the two steps over them for the last time and had a feeling that the most ordinary, helpless thing was now left alone.

One night when Susana and I spoke to him over the fence, I asked him what he was going to do when he grew up. For a moment he stayed quiet, then answered, as if finishing a very long sentence, ". . . and I'd like to be someone who always had to deliver bad news, like, for example, telling a friend that their mother has died, or telling another that they have an incurable illness. But there's no such job."

We congratulated him mockingly and promised to call on him should we hear of any misfortune, so that he could be the one to deliver the news.

When we saw him appear at the corner of Tronador, Susana and I would stare at him as he walked toward our house, since we knew it scared him enough for his firm steps to get so unsteady and awkward that he seemed about to collapse by the time he reached us. After greeting us he would go off again, as confident as he'd been at the start, but he couldn't bear to be continuously observed as he walked down the street.

One night, we saw him in the corner of our garden, hidden in the shadow of the large chinaberry trees. Determined to find out why he was hiding, we went over to say hello. He was mumbling to himself, his hands aflutter, as if emphasizing a phrase or softening a harsh word. When we asked if he was waiting for someone, he tried not to answer, but at our insistence he

116

muttered, "My sister-in-law has disappeared, and I don't know with whom. I have to break the news to my brother."

His voice betrayed such worry that to comfort him we reminded him of his wish to be the bearer of bad news, and added that perhaps a letter would be the easiest way to approach the subject.

He waited for us to finish before saying, as if remembering, "This is my first chance. I have to rehearse all the gestures. I need to savor it. I don't want to miss a single detail. In a minute, I'll go and speak to my brother."

In addition to its spaciousness, its enormous rooms, and the large garden that surrounded it, the house on Calle Tronador had two cellars beneath the dining room and the salon.

A rickety staircase led to that sliver of coolness and mystery. Among the cobwebs, piled up on bricks edged with dampened dust, were endless boxes stuffed with my father's papers, his books and manuscripts. In one corner, a few bottles brought back from Mendoza, and in another, less gloomy one, Esthercita's carriage, a trunk of her little clothes, the gown she was baptized in, and the quilt from her crib.

For us, the cellars were always the only place safe from danger, and no matter how often the years had proved the futility of that refuge, the knowledge that it was near, that its door was hidden beneath the rug, on two occasions allayed our fear of what we thought to be imminent harm.

For the few months we spent in Mendoza after my father's death, the events of the First World War were for us a hazy, distant reality, and once settled in Buenos Aires we were so cut off from all that went on in the world that we ended up forgetting it entirely.

One afternoon, rumors flew through the neighborhood that the Germans were winning. Terrified, and convinced that their victory would mean any number of humiliations, that we would be forced to marry them and to speak their language, we decided to barricade ourselves in the house. We bolted the doors and windows, lifted the trapdoor to the cellar – to allow our descent in case it were necessary – and spent all day keeping watch out of the corner of our eyes on its comforting darkness.

Three years later, we set out on that excursion into the bowels of the house for a second time. Some of the newspapers reported that, in Spain, several people had killed themselves to escape the prophecy that the world was approaching a sudden, catastrophic end. We believed it. One day, when a suicide in San Juan brought the news closer, with harrowing, fateful words, we decided to all die together and locked ourselves in the cellar. One by one, we descended into the darkness, taking what we needed to eat; but when the night, seeping into the corners, brought no omen of storm nor of hurricane, we were persuaded that it would be more convenient to perish in our respective bedrooms.

Until many years later, it was useless for us to smile at our ignorance, at our absurd, unaccustomed fears; at the slightest sign of danger we would glance at the cellar, as if that refuge shivering with cobwebs and full of damp bricks and shadows implied a constant, unchanging safety.

"Why don't you force yourself to dream?" she asked me once, under the large fig tree, as we sat and spoke of images that floated through her dreams, and the delight it gave her to know that even by night she would keep on living.

Though I was only a year older than Susana, I was the one who explained all the things she didn't understand, even though, most of the time, I didn't understand them either.

I remember, among other things, teaching her with great precision where babies came from, so that until we were both fifteen, the mystery was reduced to a simple and peaceful occurrence. Convinced that the umbilical cord was vital, it seemed logical to us that birth should occur through the belly button, and the fact that it had a kind of knot persuaded us that this need only be loosened for its folds to come undone and the baby to arrive effortlessly into the world, with no distress, with none of the agony she endured so early on. The girls in our neighborhood partook of this conviction when we explained to them, quite reasonably, that birth was just like opening a little paper candy bag tied with string, and since none of them were qualified to raise any worthwhile objection, this comforting theory remained with us until an age when others already know all there is to know.

Susana would describe her dreams with such enthusiasm that when we said good night, I would go to bed with the sorrow that, while she would be greeted by something happy, I would remain engulfed in darkness, without a single vision to steal over me in the long hours I slept so deeply.

"If you don't dream, it's the same as being dead. Why don't you force yourself to dream?"

That afternoon, as she spoke of her latest dream, I began to wonder if it was really true that by night I was dead.

But I had never dreamed before, and I felt a certain dread of rubbing shoulders with strangers as I lay in bed, not moving an arm, not opening my eyes, not saying a word.

From then on, though, I tried to quell my fear and followed Susana's advice to the letter. Before falling asleep I would think of a person, an accident, or a scene from the street, and cling to the image, trying to drag it with me into the darkness, from which I emerged the next morning as if for a few hours I had died.

Only a year later, when I was very sick, did a fever yield my first dream. On waking, I recalled something I assumed had happened the day before, but when I tried to remember, I understood that it was impossible. I called Susana and told her in a tone as joyful as hers, "Last night I dreamed Papa's dapple-gray was asleep in front of the gate. I can't remember the rest, but I know there was something behind the horse."

Susana looked at me as if I were her disciple and said condescendingly, "Tonight you'll dream again, and you'll start getting used to it . . . "

For a long time, Irene and I shared a room with two beds separated by a small table.

One night when we went to bed in high spirits, we began to talk of different things – of what we would be like in ten years' time, of our various fears. Mine were always small fears I never dared tell anyone, since I was afraid to look silly, and to be able to speak of them, I took advantage of the spells of darkness before we slept, when we seemed closer to one another than during the day.

After much trepidation (it always seemed that a fear spoken aloud might swell immeasurably, if the person in whom you confided were to add an unforeseen detail or claim it as a fear of their own), I plucked up the courage to tell her that when I turned over in bed, I always shuddered for fear that a hand might suddenly touch me in the darkness. It wasn't the intention shown by the hand that filled me with horror, or even the idea that it might try to kill me, but rather the simple fact of knowing that a strange and defenseless hand was piercing the darkness to touch me.

When I explained this to her, Irene didn't answer, and I thought, half-offended and half-relieved, that she'd nodded off. A few minutes later, I resolved to do the same, and turned to face the wall to go to sleep.

Suddenly, I felt something brush against my shoulder. A hand settled onto my own, as if it were dead. I sat up in bed with a jolt. I understood that it was Irene's hand almost straightaway, but this certainty didn't prevent my rage, or my eyes from brimming with tears. The fear I had never shared to prevent it from gaining form was now a concrete experience. Now I knew the touch of a hand in the dark.

For the first time, I thought about leaving home. It seemed dreadful that Irene had taken advantage of my trust, and I convinced myself I couldn't sleep peacefully in the same room as her for a single night. I was afraid that my fear – now out in the open – would make room for new shudders, for details until then unknown to me. But I said nothing to her.

For two or three nights, she did the same thing in the shadows. Once, she let her hand fall abruptly onto my face. I could barely contain a scream and wept in silence, musing on my chances of leaving or marrying very young.

On the fourth night, I was surprised to find that my fright had dwindled, and though I understood that Irene had inadvertently cured me, I never made her privy to any other fear.

Sometimes we spoke of how we might die of cold or heat. I would maintain that only the cold could kill me, but if my sisters asked for an explanation, I couldn't give one.

By virtue of practice, I wasn't remotely bothered when the heat was unbearable, and as far as the cold was concerned, I managed to disguise so well the trembling all of us felt on coming back from a walk that my sisters used to tell me, "You never get cold."

Whenever I could tell that my teeth were about to chatter, it was enough to lift up an arm, make any kind of gesture, or picture myself in some perilous situation for the shuddering to stop, though the cold surged through me just as intensely.

For summer days, I had other methods. While my sisters complained of the heat, I refrained from speaking and even tried to ignore them, certain that my indifference was more effective.

I spent one scorching afternoon inventing methods that might bring some relief, and came upon one that had an immediate, lasting effect: rubbing a piece of cotton against a plaster wall.

When the heat sapped us of any desire to move and we were overcome by the curious torpor of the siesta, I kept my calm as I rubbed, in my imagination, a piece of cotton against a rough wall.

The effect was immediate. One shiver after another surged through my body, goosebumps covered the skin on my arms, and a wave of coolness ran up my spine until it reached the back of my neck.

When we tried to conjure what the future had in store, she would invariably claim that all things were preordained and that she believed only in Destiny.

To support this conviction she would resort to such dangerous practical demonstrations that we often found ourselves having to contradict her.

"If I decided to stop eating I'd die of hunger, but that doesn't prove that I'm destined to die that way," one of us might argue. But she would answer that if this weren't the case, some strange force would take it upon itself to prevent the fasting. Then she would end by saying that the proof things ought to happen in one way and not the other was the very fact that they had come about that way.

It was pointless to ask her to be careful. If we said her shoelaces were undone and she might trip, she would answer, unflappable, "If I fall over, it's because I was meant to fall over. It's no use tying my shoes."

On stormy days she would go out into the street, lean against a tree and watch the sky as if she'd decided to defy it, paying no heed at all to the thunder or lightning.

She was so fragile that it made us sad to see her court all kinds of danger, laughing off superstitions – which for us were hidden and helpful warnings – stopping beneath scaffolding, crossing the street without paying attention to traffic, convinced that nothing could interfere with her destiny.

The last time I saw her she looked so gaunt it was impossible not to suggest she should take better care of herself. She answered in a bitter, rebellious tone that this would solve nothing, that it was too late; and no matter how much we spoke of her health, at every moment she avoided the word Destiny.

Elvira Cabral, you had all that you needed to be happy: your smooth brow, broad smile, subtle hair, and small eyes. You seemed at ease wherever you found yourself. When we sat together at school, the urge to fidget and shout always overcame me. You sat still, in your big starched pinafore. Your handwriting was slender and straight. I sat with you and was sometimes ashamed that I couldn't concentrate on the book, couldn't listen to the other girls without interrupting them. You looked at me and protested solemnly, "Let them finish. It'll be your turn soon," not knowing that what drove me wasn't impatience, but rather the will to burst in and stir up trouble, to be troublesome.

You never blushed. You never brought the teacher flowers. This was the only thing we had in common. I was as horrified as you by the bouquets other girls presented. You watched them in silence and your gaze met mine as if saying, "Enough!"

If you left early, I hated asking anyone else for a pencil or a piece of paper. When I was left alone, the other girls begged me to tell mischievous tales. When you were nearby, I agreed, knowing that you disliked them; but after you left, it seemed more proper not to take advantage of your absence, avoiding the reproach of your big starched white pinafore.

One afternoon, the teacher read us a section from Juan Ramón Jiménez, and you began to take notice of me for the first time. It was a page from *Platero and I*. Neither of us knew anything of literature, but for the first time, our expressions were identical.

Your big white pinafore moved a bit closer to me. Neat and spotless, you used to remind me of a sewing basket with so many pockets for everything. Your big starched pinafore, bright and cool, with its placid, slender panels, was the most appealing thing about you. As if you had only just put it on, its frosty stiffness added to its pallor the sad, strained look of wax flowers.

You looked just like yourself all year, as if every morning in class were your first. You never brought candies, or anything that might detract from your air of readiness for the day, the night, or the rest of your life.

Before we parted at the end of the year, we tried writing some poems in a classmate's yearbook. You wrote a stanza that I found touching. I told you this, just as I told you everything, brimming with enthusiasm, unruliness. You read mine and only as you were leaving, as we said goodbye, did you remark solemnly, "You chose the most difficult thing, what I would like to be when I grow up. But I've got it all worked out."

All I could do was bid you goodbye. Wouldn't you always be right, one way or another?

How many times must the meaning of a phrase have escaped me due to my habit of counting the syllables while someone was speaking! If my fingers reached the count of ten I felt great relief, since otherwise I had to keep time until the phrase ended on the twentieth or thirtieth syllable. In the beginning, I repeated the first few words, though the voice of the person speaking might have already followed a different course or changed its tempo. But once the ten-syllable phrase was done, I let go of my habit and could listen in peace.

Whenever Mother scolded me, my fingers would start to move almost imperceptibly, and this invisible game would sap her words of their force. One afternoon, someone said to me, "At long last, you are going to arrive." The brief phrase paused on my fingers. Its intimate meaning – struggling, breathing – and its truth or falsehood were neither important nor lofty beside my delight, as my fingers, more accustomed by now than my ear, collected it perfect and intact.

But poetry did not stir me to study or scan it. My fingers moved only when someone spoke to me, and they were soon so nimble that I could follow whole conversations by counting the syllables on them. It was just that I was excluded. When I realized this, too late, I had to try all kinds of gestures to keep my hands from idleness, and gradually lose the habit of that engrossing pastime.

Later, just occasionally, my fingers would run through the ten syllables of a phrase and rest upon it, as if possessing it forever. But by then I was listening to it, too.

For a long time, we were the only family on Calle Tronador with a telephone. If anyone in the neighborhood needed one, they had to go to the grocery store, or ask to use ours.

There came a time, however, when we decided to refuse permission, since the oddest people would come to our house. But one of us would often assent to a stranger's request without telling the others, so as we crossed the drawing room, we would frequently bump into someone unawares, peeking slyly into the rooms as if planning to rob us, or a gruff voice would burst into the bedrooms, waking us up with a start. At other times we would offer to pass on a message, but we always disliked this since we were afraid the time would come when we would have to deliver some serious news and we might not know how.

One afternoon, I was asked to call the Spanish Hospital to inquire about a neighbor's son. When I learned of his death, I lingered beside the phone, unable to decide whether to break the news in person or send someone else who might do it more artfully.

In an attempt to sway myself, I tried to remember something about his life – a gesture, a phrase steeped in sadness – but only his most comical movements came to mind, the outline of his clumsy, ungainly figure. I tried to rehearse a grief-stricken air, but I was convinced that even if my sorrow were genuine, the look on my face could never convey it.

I put off the news as long as I could and decided to look for Susana. The fear all five of us shared of not knowing what to say at solemn moments – which was to haunt us even at times of truly boundless pain – gave me little expectation of any help she might offer. But when I told her of the death, Susana guessed what I was thinking and said immediately, "Remember the way he drank water? It made you so impatient!"

I soon pictured him sitting at the table with a glass of water in front of him, and remembered that because he disliked cold water he would spend a long time warming the glass in his hands, as I have since seen people do with cognac.

This detail was enough for me to feel sure of myself, and decide to deliver the news.

When she played the piano, knowing like us that sooner or later it too would be sold, she rested her fingers gently on its keys, but with the urgency of someone who drinks without thirst, sensing that water will soon be scarce.

We would stand quietly beside her as she improvised, and began to notice a thin patch in her hair, and perhaps because of this detail or the soft, poignant music she played that saddened us so, at these times we loved her more than ever.

I don't know which of us spoke for the first time of her hair. The deaths of my father and Esthercita had given her an absentminded look, so the time when she couldn't countenance a shabby ribbon, a wave out of place in her coiffure, was now so distant it seemed like a dream.

Accustomed to her neatness and beauty, we rebelled against the advent of this weariness, and were distressed to think this tendency toward resignation and neglect might become even more pronounced.

One day, when we came upon her in front of the mirror, she announced that her hair was falling out. We evoked the change in season and who knows what other weather-related excuses, even though we sensed that autumn would last a long time, and that the lie would not endure.

Week after week, her dark waves grew gradually sparser and sparser, until one night, slightly in jest and slightly in sorrow,

134

she took from a drawer a long braid of her own hair, which at one time she had worn coiled around her head.

"I'm going to wear it," she said with a smile, as if hoping our words would convince her there wasn't yet any need. The braid looked so young and fresh to us that we agreed, and when we asked her to unfasten it, the hair floated about as if someone had suddenly opened a window. But the sorrow of the empty bedroom, of her worn-out dress, of what we were still unable to give her, of what had slipped through her hands and away before her eyes, rose up in pure anguish behind our gestures and our words.

"Why don't you wear it undone? When your hair grows back, you can take it off. No one will notice, and anyway, it's yours."

"I had been thinking that," she answered, her voice full of jumbled memories.

Tossed onto the bed, the braid looked like a final gesture, a decision, a farewell. From time to time, one of us would run a hand over its smooth, cold waves. Someone tried it on. The almost black braid looked strange against her fair hair, and we laughed. The feeling was drained from her words, as was a little of her fear.

Years later, when she sat down at the piano we all gave her, there was no sparseness that could trouble us, nor any foreboding that could shake our affection.

By repeating it to myself and confirming its easy comfort, I ended up solving all my problems with the simple, idle thought, "Whatever happens, when tonight comes, I'll be asleep."

In this way, when making conjectures about the future, I found solace in the certainty that if I could find no one to marry, it would be enough to fall asleep and forget about everything, and I plotted long stretches of slumber that would shorten my life, allowing me to reach – without having wholly lived, and without my presence being too noted – the age when no one expects anything of us.

This efficient method of avoiding woe accompanied me in the widest range of circumstances, at times when I could find nothing to hold on to, such as, for example, while I waited my turn at the dentist's office. As I heard the machine's hum, and the pointed silence before a nerve extraction, I would fix my gaze on the clock to memorize the exact duration of one, five, or ten minutes, and repeat to myself: "In forty, ninety moments identical to this one, it will all have passed and I'll be asleep."

I never foresaw insomnia, the angst that might provoke it or which might not fade with sleep. But a few years later the nights began to lengthen until my belief was shattered, and when I confronted my first sorrow, my first true and turbulent fear, I understood all the reasons why I had evaded this knowledge in such a way.

It was the second night that from my bed I had heard the door
to the garden open and the same cautious steps retreat from
my window. As if that mysterious departure through the door
nearest the street entailed a danger, a new and unfamiliar
world in the life of one of my sisters, I had stayed awake and
waited for her return.

That night, unable to guess who it was, I decided to try
and find out. I waited for the steps to vanish at the bottom
of the garden, then got up with the utmost caution and,
wrapped in a dark blanket, went out into the courtyard lit
by a full moon.

The large chinaberry trees on Calle Tronador traced enormous paths of gloom on the walls of the house. I crouched
down and inched forward, trying not to let my shadow lengthen
too much, then took refuge behind a palm tree. From there
I could see the bottom of the garden and both sides of the
house.

Though the moon lit the way around the slightest bends in
the path, I caught no glimpse of anyone, anywhere. I assumed
the steps had headed toward the street, but the padlock was
in its usual place on the gate.

Suddenly, I saw a silhouette move in the brightest patch
of the garden. Leaning against a tree, she was wrapped in a
voluminous poncho that had belonged to my father. For a few

seconds, she gazed up at the sky, then opened her arms and slipped out of it.

Naked, silent, motionless, her body shone against the darkest part of the tree's thick trunk. She remained like this, without a shiver, for a few minutes, as if she were waiting for something. When she leaned down to pick up the poncho I hurried back to my room, and, once in bed, heard her stealthy steps and the door close softly.

The next night, hidden behind the palm tree, I saw her leaning against a tree trunk again, completely naked, shimmering in the moonlight. But scarcely a minute had passed when I sensed a man come whistling down Calle Tronador. When he reached the edge of our railings, the whistling stopped. I was about to cry in fright that she should cover herself, even though it was impossible for her to be seen from the street. But she too had heard, and hurriedly picked up the poncho and went inside.

Though I stayed up for many nights after, the scene was never repeated.

One day when I was looking for a book in Marta's bedroom, among her things I came across a technique for acquiring beauty. A few sheets of folded paper described a formula that involved going outside naked on a night with a full moon. All you had to do to become irresistibly seductive was spend a few minutes completely caressed by the cold moonlight. Clearly, by bathing in moonlight three nights in a row, Marta had hoped to intensify its effect.

One night, Irene discovered that in the dark I almost always discreetly reached out from the covers to line up my shoes under the bed. My annoyance at the certainty that not a day or night would go by without them getting knocked out of place – one of those obsessions that was impossible to give up – was so much worsened by her mocking attitude that I was sometimes afraid I might end up hating her.

When we went to bed, I was the one who turned out the light, and while Irene smoked a cigarette in the dark I could tidy my shoes in peace.

In the morning, however, it was impossible to prevent Irene's foot, sometimes by accident, but almost always on purpose, from kicking one of my shoes as she removed a dress from the wardrobe beside my bed, in her typical morning ill humor. I didn't need to watch to know if it was intentional or not, and would wordlessly clench my teeth, pretend to be asleep, or cry silently until she left and I could put it back in its place.

Convinced that any explanation, any plea, would be useless, in the end I tried to arouse her compassion. I told her that, though it might seem silly, her attitude was enough to sour a whole day for me, and that she was to blame for my many sleepless nights. Her apparently sincere contrition led me to believe I'd managed to soften her with my words, but the next morning she began her exasperating game all over again.

Only after a long while could I explain her unease and ill humor. She had to get up several hours before I did. Once our schedules began to coincide, the row of shoes remained in order under the bed.

On many days, he stayed in bed, and when I asked if he'd slept well, his answers were always so odd that, on hearing them, I couldn't rid myself of the certainty that he was being untruthful.

"Last night I flew a kite and it flapped so hard I was almost dragged along with it. I'm so exhausted, I'm going to stay in bed today."

I kept my comments to myself, and left his room a little impatiently.

When he felt better, he spent nearly all of his time in the street. He was eighteen and, as far as we knew, his only joy was helping the neighborhood children make kites; but his weakness scarcely allowed him to hold on to them, and once they took flight, or if they ever broke free or fell in a tangle, he would go to his room, and for a long time we wouldn't see him. He enjoyed this pastime, as much as it grieved him to see a torn kite caught in a treetop.

One afternoon, once again in his bed, he assembled an enormous green kite. He stuck many hexagonal papers together with a thick paste, then suddenly leaned back, closed his eyes, and said the windows were too small, that he was suffocating.

When they lifted the kite that almost engulfed the whole bed, he had already breathed his last.

No matter the pecuniary troubles that plagued us all day long, the garden had only to fill with shadows for us to escape them, and, gathered in the arbor, we keenly lived the final hours still separating us from that lovely, mysterious stretch of time we shared in the darkness.

One night as our dreams drifted apart until we all seemed suddenly different, Marta asked Mother how a woman could tell when she loved a man.

Always willing to answer with a seriousness I discovered only much later, Mother said with a smile, "It's very easy. Just imagine him in the most grotesque situations you can. Perched naked on the wall and singing, for example. If he passes that test without causing you any repulsion, then it's true love."

We laughed and began to imagine the men we knew in the silliest outfits and situations. None of them seemed able to withstand being caught in an inappropriate position.

Suddenly, as if we'd enveloped her in expectant silence, or as if the same question had just arisen in all of us, Georgina asked, "When you fell in love with Papa, did you have to imagine him a thousand different ways to know if you loved him?"

"There was no need," Mother answered, in a tone of such pride and reproach that we were all overcome with shame.

At one time, it occurred to me to make a list of my obsessions, to contemplate them coldly and perhaps try to free myself of one. Though I understood that the most stubborn were rooted in my early years, I decided to combat the more recent ones. But this premature study brought me no rest, and for a long time I continued to envy my sisters, who didn't waste even a minute when they went to bed, while I spent whole hours on pointless comings and goings that never brought me any relief.

When I performed a task neatly, it wasn't due to my meticulousness but to an obsessive desire to ensure the well-being of any object, and, if possible, for it to be touching another, similar one. Colored pencils, clippings of words, and toys could never be lonely, since they were always placed beside one another, as if talking secretly.

I remember that the governess taught us always to tidy our clothes. I would lay the nightgowns one on top of the other, trying to prevent them from brushing against the panties. I could never bear to leave a petticoat all by itself, far from the others, since it seemed to me that this made it feel forlorn.

Before going to bed, we had to put our toys in their place. It wasn't enough for me to gather the dolls together, to give them enough affection by making their arms touch one another. I also took care to arrange their poses. Sometimes, at night, I had to get up and go secretly into the playroom to make sure none of them still had an arm held high, a head hanging low or twisted backward. I wouldn't have been able to sleep, thinking of how she would spend all night with a bent leg, sitting sideways in an uncomfortable position. For a long time, this habit remained with me. Later, whenever I stayed at a house with small children, I would wait until they were tucked in to secretly visit the dolls, and, with a distracted gesture, lower an arm or straighten a leg.

It was also impossible for me to take just one sip of water, or any other drink. It had to be two, four, or six. Even when I had to take medicine in one gulp, no matter how nasty it tasted, I would separate it into two in my mouth. It was the same with beer. No matter how thirsty I was, I would count the sips as I drank, always ending on an even number, and for a long time, every night, I drank four little sips of water before going to bed.

Of the years at Calle Tronador, there are few things I wish to forget, since time has softened their bitter and painful edges. But no distance can lessen one displeasure I endured for two years: the fold-up bed.

Since all the bedrooms were occupied, I had to sleep in the big salon, which preserved the sense of that comforting name only in its size. To give it a cozier air, Mother had placed an enormous screen – another mortifying contraption – in the corner facing the one occupied by the piano, and behind the screen stood my fold-up bed.

Each night, before I went to sleep, I had to draw back the screen to open my bed. This operation – enough to induce any kind of insomnia in itself – would inevitably put me in a bad mood. I couldn't stop thinking of how I was sleeping all alone, and that each night the improvised bed robbed sleep of its seriousness. It was humiliating to sleep in a bed made to be rolled up with its covers – with me inside it, as soon as I let down my guard – and I shuddered at the mere idea of being taken ill in front of a guest, and of someone bringing the mobile bed to me, as if it were acceptable not to seek out a respectable bed oneself instead.

In the morning, when the bed disappeared behind the screen I felt great relief, but if we had guests and played hide-and-seek or truth or dare, its secret existence made me uneasy once again. I was sure no one would hesitate to hide behind the screen, and when they discovered the bed – barely higher than an icebox – and asked who it was who dared to sleep there, my sisters would betray me in their usual irritating tone.

A year later, Mother bought me a divan in a sale. It arrived just in time, since I had to spend several weeks in bed, and I winced with shame to imagine the doctor examining me in that improper, improvised, humiliating fold-up bed.

When the divan was delivered and I stretched out in that modest but unconvertible, definitive bed for the first time, I felt overcome with happiness.

One afternoon, when she came to have tea as usual, we began to make fun of her and tried to convince her that she was cold, and that, despite her engagement, she was incapable of passion, or of behaving as we imagined that women in love should behave. She objected a little awkwardly that not everyone expressed themselves in the same way, and though she did indeed love a great deal, she preferred not to make a show of it.

Endeavoring to prolong the joke, we kept trying to come up with a phrase that included "flesh," to give her a nickname that implied flesh and coldness at once.

"Withered flesh, smooth flesh," Marta listed.

Determined to find the right term, and latching onto the first that came into my head, I cried, "Slow flesh," and all of us chanted, "Slow flesh" in a gleeful voice.

That afternoon, she went out into the garden, and treated the fiancé who'd come to meet her more coolly than ever. When they went toward the arbor, we decided to get closer and, disregarding her modesty, passed close by them several times. One of us whispered, "Slow flesh," but she pretended not to have heard, and as she bid us goodbye she gave us a kiss as she always did, with not a shred of bitterness to cool her embrace.

One month before the date of the wedding, her fiancé had an accident that made it necessary to amputate his leg. We suspected that perhaps she might leave him, that she would find an excuse for them not to marry. But quite the opposite happened; they never parted.

Only once did we call her "Slow flesh" again. Though she wasn't there, we suddenly realized we'd been unfair, and the nickname returned to our mouths in the low tone of a harsh reproach.

Once the problem of the chickens had been ruled out, other obstacles arose, so difficult to overcome that I ended up convinced that the only solution was to remain a spinster.

It was enough to imagine the moment my husband would take off his socks for a shiver to run down my spine. I felt not so much repulsion but fear that something might be wrong with his feet, or that the gesture would be so unfortunate that I would stop loving him. I suspected that one night, after inspecting his feet, he would remark on his observations, the drawbacks of his new boots, or the changeable weather. Although I had daily proof of the discretion between my sisters and me, I convinced myself that conjugal intimacy meant accepting many dubious things and that nothing could ever be concealed from the other, so I peppered Mother with questions and for a long time couldn't stop fretting, despite her calm answers and the giggles of all my sisters.

My irritation at any mention of feet led me to think of those who might have been able to speak of them without my affections cooling, but it was enough to imagine an engineer, a family friend, risking such an allusion to rid him of his air of mystery and refinement.

There was, however, a far more serious problem: the nose.

It wasn't its shape or respiratory purpose that mattered to me, but rather how often some men touch, refer to, and stroke it meditatively. One of my greatest fears was that a young man I knew might use the excuse of a nasal mishap not to visit, since although it might not have bothered me if he didn't come, I would have felt humiliated to receive a message explaining an absence in such a way.

The nose of a woman or a child, squashed white against a window – celebrated all too often by moviegoers – so disgusted me that the mere suggestion of a favorite actress making the gesture was enough for my admiration of her to immediately plummet.

I am not aware of the advantage of those who didn't suffer the small fears that roamed through my childhood, but I know these fears swayed my preferences to the point of dissolving an early courtship.

He had been visiting our house for several months, and one afternoon when we were left alone he asked me for a pencil and paper to copy down a poem he wanted to give me.

He sat at the table and tried to recall the beginning, while I, on the other side, contemplated his large face, his sad and slender hands. Suddenly, a wave of anger forced me to stand up so as not to see him.

As he rested his chin on the palm of his hand, he had lifted his middle finger and placed it on the end of his nose. I could tell what was going to happen immediately. It wasn't enough for him to rest his finger there; he gradually pushed it upward, making his nostrils stretch and the tip of his nose pale around the place where his finger pressed.

The gesture lasted mere seconds – but long enough for me to be permanently disappointed and to feel great relief when he announced he was going to leave.

It wasn't enough for him to roll his eyes constantly. Each look caused a simultaneous turn of his head, as if his milky eyes wished to leave nothing unseen.

In the end, this constant tilting irritated me in a way that was difficult to contain.

"Can't you look at anything without turning your head?" I would ask, unable to imagine he didn't know how to do so properly at the age of sixteen.

On nights when we would all meet in the plaza, he would challenge me to guess the number on a streetcar more than eight blocks away. It was pointless to squint at the glowing sign; I could never make out the number until long after he announced it. It didn't take me long to realize, though, that the position of the lights allowed him to see them from afar.

Once, I asked him how he got ready for bed and whether he stayed still when he was asleep.

"I get scared," he answered curtly, in a thin voice. "They say if you stare at something, it ends up haunting you. That's why I look at things out of the corner of my eye, and as soon as I see one thing, I move on to the next right away."

"Not everything you see can haunt you," I answered. "At the most, one or two things might – the cat, a person . . . "

"One or two . . . " he said with a smile, and went off saying "One or two . . . " over and over.

When the time came for his military service, the doctors examined his eyes and declared him exempt.

Not only I but also my sisters and the neighbors had all believed he had supernatural vision. In fact, he turned out to be almost blind.

Six young people around a table. Six grown stomachs surrounding a tablecloth, with no food there to offer its comforting presence.

Eduardo, my sisters and I all searched each other's faces for a lapse in anyone's appetite. But we were all hungry, and our hunger endured, intact and absolute.

That day, it was my turn for the "extra" helping. When I remember, I shudder to think of how we would get up at the crack of dawn to be met with what we knew wouldn't be enough, and rush to the meager, fleeting comfort of the extra helping.

In the next room, someone was slicing loaves of Vienna bread fresh out of the oven, spreading them with lard.

Around the table, the other five discreetly awaited my hunger's decision. Would I accept or not? It was my turn that morning! They sat down to drink their coffee and milk, scarcely a piece of bread to go with it, and I approached my seat with determination. The "extra" helping consisted of crumbs that fell from the loaves when they were sliced. We would pile them onto a small plate, sprinkle them with sugar, and serve ourselves with a teaspoon to make them last longer. Since there were six of us, we each had one turn a week.

We were almost never generous enough to alter the pre-established order. As I kept the barely appetizing crumbs in my mouth, I suspected the others were lowering their gaze so as not to disturb me with their expressive eyes.

We were modest in our hunger. If we didn't sometimes give up that "extra" helping it was out of modesty, modesty on behalf of the one who would have to hide their enthusiasm. Our hunger was a demure hunger. A well-mannered hunger.

Later, the extra helping was retired. We discovered that the bread from the day before was more accessible and took up more space in our bellies. The little breadcrumbs disappeared from the menu.

But in another part of the house, someone kept on breaking loaves of Vienna bread into pieces, and that sole gesture, with all its mysterious cracking, filled us with hatred.

One night I thought out of nowhere how terrible it would be if I found myself unable to resist the urge to tell one of my friends that her mother was stupid, or that her favorite sister deserved to be called a nobody or a fool. But to tell her calmly, neither using an apologetic tone nor basing my claim on any argument; in the simplest, most plainspoken way, while we took tea in front of everyone, as if it had only just occurred to me. After a while I stopped thinking about this nonsense and fell asleep, but a few days later, during a visit Susana and I paid to some dear friends, I was suddenly gripped by the temptation to declare that the owner of the house was an idiot.

I felt the urge become irrepressible, and a strange sensation of shame and fear rose up my legs. While the others chattered and laughed, I waited for the right moment to say "Your father is an idiot" just as serenely as when one comes to a conclusion about anything else.

By virtue of restraint, and telling myself over and over that only I deserved to be called such a thing, I managed to keep the urge in check, but to feel some relief, I had to take advantage of a moment of hubbub to say, "Your father," and finish the sentence in any way at all.

Sometimes, I would get up and lock myself in the bathroom to whisper what some inner force tried to compel me to say aloud. At other times I would change the name, and instead of saying, "Your mother is ugly," I would say, "Whatshisname is ugly," or, "Your mother has a marvelous sense of humor." Often, when I had named someone, the obsession would quieten until it disappeared completely. Once calm, I felt full of sorrow and on the verge of tears.

We used to see her pass nervously, hurrying briskly home from school. Sometimes she talked to herself, while at others she stared at the ground, looking lost in thought. Her house was next to ours, and from among the large fig trees at the bottom of the garden, we could hear her mother's constant recriminations.

One afternoon, when we were playing hide-and-seek, I hid behind some sheets of tin leaning against the side wall. While the others were searching for me, I heard a cry and a phrase I couldn't banish from my mind for the rest of the day. It was the girl we saw pass by every afternoon. She must have been tormented, I know not by what terrible visions, and her voice hoarse with fear forced me out of my hiding place. My sisters had also heard and we all began to listen, huddled against the wall so we couldn't be seen.

"Starve me! Beat me all you want, but don't lock me in the dark! Please don't lock me in the dark!"

We heard a sharp slap and made out another, more distant cry, "Don't lock me in the dark!"

Then there was a long silence. By now she must have been plunged into loneliness. Out of pity, moved by the fear that made her voice quaver, we decided to intervene. We clapped our hands several times and, when no one came, began to throw stones at the house. When she heard them bounce off the tin roof, the woman appeared in a fury.

Irene asked her as sweetly as she possibly could why she didn't inflict a different punishment on her daughter since her fear of the dark might be harmful, but the woman objected angrily.

"I know what I'm doing. I'm her mother, after all."

The next day, when I saw her come home from school, I went over to her and said, "You mustn't despair if they lock you in a dark room. Nothing will happen to you. It's just like having your eyes closed. When your mother realizes it no longer scares you, she won't lock you in anymore. You should pretend it doesn't bother you, even if you're scared to death."

"I will," she answered, in a voice so terrified by the mere thought of the punishment that I decided to lie and tell her that after punishing me that way, my parents had given up when they realized what little effect it had.

As I was going to bed that night I thought of the darkness, and for the first time I was afraid. But I resolved to conduct an experiment to see if the fear would turn to terror, or if it was possible to get used to it. I closed the doors and imagined myself roaming around the room, searching for a way out, or at least a crack that would let in a beam of light.

For a moment, my fear obscured the little triangle of light coming through the keyhole. I tried to calm down, to overcome my anxiety. In desperation, I tiptoed around the furniture, whose position I remembered perfectly, and with a sigh of relief, I opened the door.

When I was ten, I stopped praying, though I don't know why. But when I learned at Tronador that the others had continued, I began to say Our Fathers and Ave Marias again.

One night I thought, given that I never went to mass, that I ought to be making more of a sacrifice, so I decided to pray kneeling down next to my pillow. But since Irene and I shared a room, I had to be quick and pray in the dark so she wouldn't see me.

As I got into the habit of praying, the list of people for whom I begged or gave thanks grew longer. I prayed for my mother, for my sisters – that they should marry –, for the mortgaged plots of land in Mendoza, for the elderly newspaper saleswoman at the station . . . and for the world not to come to a catastrophic end, since in those days there was a rumor that some people had killed themselves rather than wait for such a prophecy to be fulfilled. Later, I divided the list into three different parts: one for those in my house, one for the most urgent things, and one for things whose solution might take a long time; but I rarely managed to keep my calm, since I had to keep a constant watch on Irene so she wouldn't catch me.

Later, even this position seemed too comfortable, so I decided to kneel on the floor. The fear that someone might see me stopped me from praying calmly, despite the knowledge that all five of us shared this reserve.

On rare occasions when we all had to cross ourselves at once, we always tried to do so while the others weren't looking. We stopped going to mass, mostly for fear of conducting ourselves incorrectly, of kneeling at the wrong time, of someone giving us a mocking look, of one of us getting the idea to spy on the others.

One morning after dressing to go out and catch the train, I kneeled down beside my bed to pray, and heard Georgina turning the door handle. Without a moment's hesitation, I threw myself onto the floor and pretended to have dropped something under the bed. Georgina must have suspected what had happened, because I blushed. But she never said a word.

One afternoon when we came home from school, we saw someone arguing with our mother. He looked at the piano so covetously that we soon realized the reason for his visit; a few days earlier, a visit from another person of the same sort had coincided with the disappearance of our washing machine.

When the man left, Mother said in a voice more steeped in weariness than ever, "I've decided to sell the piano."

Together, we all sensed that the worst was to come, since though we'd suspected it many times, the sale of the piano was something we didn't dare countenance for even an instant. The side table, the enormous mirror in the drawing room, and nearly all the furniture we brought from Mendoza had already gone, but giving up the piano represented a decisive, unmistakable poverty. Not even the sale of a large part of the garden had saddened us so much, since there was still no fence to divide us from its familiar trees, its darkest corners. Resigning ourselves to the piano's absence was different; the piano was all that was unconcerned with poverty, the only thing that allowed us to forget certain unpleasant but necessary daily chores like washing the dishes, cooking, and making the beds. One after another, we used to play a few pieces with the windows open, convinced that the neighbors would come out onto the path to hear us.

161

That night, we decided we'd each play a piece to bid it farewell. Mother played before anyone else, but her fingers trailed across the keys until she suddenly stopped, claiming she felt unmoved. Irene and Marta spent only a few minutes. Then Georgina, who knew more music than the rest of us, played. My turn was next, and I was the last.

When I sat down at the piano, it seemed to me that no other farewell could reach that tone of lament, that definitive sadness. The others had all withdrawn, and I kept on playing for a long time, one piece after another, just as I often used to so they could hear me from their beds. Without any shame, I noticed a tear tremble on the keys, and watched as it rolled down in between them.

The next morning, a truck came to take it away. Gathered in their doorways, as if it were a burial, the neighbors remarked on its removal. Behind the curtains, not daring to go out into the street, we gazed at the black, silent, glossy piano, until it was draped in canvas and loaded onto the truck.

We soon saw Mother head into her room with something balled up in her hand. A while later, when we went into the salon, one of us tried to make a joke on seeing that the empty space was covered in dust and cobwebs. We silently put on our white pinafores and set off for school. Mother remained alone in front of the rectangle of dust.

Until the age of thirteen, I lived by a code of honor that allowed for no exceptions, though the desire to satisfy a minor revenge could tempt me to defy it. Nevertheless, I was always held back by the certainty that I might harm more than just my intended target. This reasoning applied only to certain dietary needs that were all too often thwarted by the dogs' food.

Marta was more astute than I, and didn't think food worth fighting for, so she would pass the dogs with a tired, indifferent air. But when I spied them guarding the gate or curled up drowsing after a feast, I would feel as if a fist were knocking against my insides.

It wasn't that I didn't love them. The largest one looked like a black calf, and when it returned from an adventure and placed its enormous, hot, filthy paws on my shoulders, it warmed my heart. I was less fond of the other, a sheepdog, which reminded us of daughters born to large families just as they begin to prosper, who take piano lessons and attend the School for Young Ladies, whose first names are typically shortened and whose last are triple-barreled.

They had come to our house with some relatives who lived with us for two years.

At ten in the morning and five in the afternoon, an overwhelming aversion would keep me away from the dogs. This was when they scarfed down two liters of milk and a kilo of bread, the same flaky bread I still enjoy to this day. We had to witness the spectacle over and over, while trying to distract the anguish of an appetite hardened by the frequent absence of food.

In these moments, honor was a virtue hard to endure, and I would have liked to steal some bread, but only so long as the dogs' owners discovered the theft, since otherwise much of the scheme's interest would have been lost.

Meanwhile, Marta's indolence and exasperation had a small vengeance in store that we all looked forward to equally.

We had arranged to take turns cleaning the kitchen, our utensils, and those of our relatives for a week. When Irene, Georgina, Susana, and I were in charge of the task, we knew the crockery would not be significantly diminished, but when Marta's turn came, we could predict what would happen.

We knew that to calm her aversion to a task that was always monstrous and repetitive to us, little by little, with systematic apathy, without making a scene or shouting or refusing to do her duty, one by one, she would drop the plates, glasses, and cups. When she'd managed to reduce the collection to the bare minimum, she said without a hint of malice and with no apparent gratification, "There are eleven dinner plates, eleven dessert dishes, and the same number of cups and glasses. The same goes for the silverware. This morning I dropped three spoons into the well and couldn't get them out. Do me a favor and be careful."

Once she had carried out the first part of her plan, with the same cool and impassive air she taught the dogs – too aristocratic for leftovers – to lick the dirty plates. One by one she would line up the dishes, and the dogs, drawn to the novel flavor, would lick them until they were shiny, and Marta would place them carefully under the flowing tap.

Today, I suspect that what I mistook for resentment was in fact misery. Her system achieved at least one unforeseen goal: the dogs loved her, though they did not understand her.

When our appetite stirred our imagination, Susana, Eduardo and I would get together to work out the easiest way to acquire a few coins. Our older sisters weren't involved in these pressing matters, nor were they aware, like us, of the value of empty bottles, broken pipes, and hats no longer worn, nor could they recognize to which category the buyer's cry belonged when it echoed down the block.

We, on the other hand, knew how to appraise at first glance a faucet in poor condition, a shaky partition wall that might render a saleable truss, the resources a forgotten overcoat in a trunk in the cellar might yield.

But this method of banishing hunger caused two disappointments that forced us, to our regret, to abandon these schemes for acquiring food.

Our first brush with sullen faces and recriminations came when we heard the voice of the old man who bought old shoes for one and a half pesos per kilo. We went out to offer him some magnificent ladies' boots which had cost forty-five pesos, and for which we received the handsome sum of one sixty-five.

The second was a result of our culinary generosity, which moved us to arrange for our family to enjoy some boiled eggs.

The neighbor in the back had a henhouse well stocked with laying hens, separated from our garden by a wall that just reached our shoulders. One afternoon when their cheerful clucking reverberated in our stomachs with fierce and tempting nostalgia, we decided to implement a plan we'd postponed several times.

Armed with a cane to which we'd tied a small tin that swayed on the end of a piece of string, when we heard the first cluck we climbed onto the garden wall and lowered the container. A single jerk was enough for the egg to roll into the tin with ease.

The hens didn't observe a fixed schedule, so we obtained only half a dozen eggs in the two hours we spent on our scheme. But the task couldn't have been easier since they took it upon themselves to announce the moment they'd just laid an egg.

Within a week, we managed to fish nearly all the eggs out of the henhouse, but the clucking that had been so beneficial ruined our system. Tired of heeding the absurd call and finding no trace of anything worthwhile, the neighbor suspected something unusual was going on, since such a coordinated ploy on the part of the chickens seemed unlikely.

One morning as we were coaxing an egg into the tin by means of a thousand stratagems, the neighbor burst out, red-faced, from behind a crate. That very afternoon, a chicken-wire fence was erected and cut us off from our wholesome pastime forever.

At fourteen, one of my favorite hobbies was to shout my head off, and once I couldn't go on, to laugh; I laughed slowly at first, and then grew louder, until my shrieks echoed all along the block. Susana and Eduardo would join me in spending whole afternoons in the doorways of neighboring houses, laughing until the inhabitants begged us to make ourselves scarce.

At other times, I would put on a man's felt hat, and, bundled up in a poncho, climb onto the kitchen roof, from which I could see into the surrounding houses. I would throw a few bricks at the roofs to get the neighbors' attention, then begin my speech.

After hollering two or three words in different languages, I would call all the neighbors by their names in a booming voice, and when a few suspicious heads began to peer up at me, my voice and gestures became so forceful that my cries reverberated against the doors, the windowpanes, and the zinc roofs.

Sometimes inquiring, sometimes ironic, my expletives were followed by paragraphs in English and French, disjointed sentences, the name of some neighbor or other, the few words I knew in Italian or Norwegian, collective insults, a raucous guffaw, an affected line of verse. If a neighbor gave in to the temptation to chide me or to applaud, the insults, my flawed polyglossia, my random gesticulations, and the thuds against the zinc roofs would rain down even harder.

When I suspected my cries would soon refuse to emerge from my mouth, I would perform some balancing exercises on the garden wall to begin part two of my routine. Without altering my composure, a scarcely audible laughter would gradually turn into one guffaw after another, a barrage as thunderous as a stampede, at which today I can't help but smile.

Wrapped in the poncho, red in the face, the hat pulled down to my eyes, I unflappably pursued this task, which would go on for over an hour, until, having lost my voice, I descended gravely and locked myself in my room.

No matter how hard he tried to hold his head up straight, it always leaned to one side. Too big and too pale, he seemed fatigued by his back, his arms, and his round blue eyes, which were colder than his calm and slightly clammy skin.

On some afternoons, his mother would let me watch over him, until little by little she got used to leaving him in my care. His gaze, the rare seriousness with which he came to me, was far more appealing than any other distraction. When he rested his large head in my arms for hours on end my back would stiffen, but I felt so grateful for his weariness that to prolong it I would delay the moment I laid him down as long as I could, as if staying for a long time in an uncomfortable position in bed, to savor the moment of turning over. But once he fell asleep, the same fear always overcame me: I imagined his head might get so heavy that he would fall from my arms.

For the whole time I watched over him during meals, I made only one mistake in my affection, burning him slightly on the mouth. I imagined that he would suffer all night, that he might even die, that, rather than a reproach, cloaked in his small, almost silent cries was a hidden sorrow.

A few months later, his father banished me from the house; his exceptional insight into facial features had persuaded him that my mouth showed certain signs of latent evil.

His house was scarcely a block from ours. In vain he would gaze at me from the gate with his large, round blue eyes that now looked even colder. I had to pass by without pausing and watch him from afar, or spy him on the balcony when I climbed up onto the wall around our house on sunny mornings.

One afternoon, he spoke of serious things, and asked for white roses to be brought to his room. His large head – his head that had never been fevered – lay on the bed.

When they called me to see him and I stood before the little white coffin, I experienced for the first time a sense of injustice. His father was there, but I said nothing to him. I remembered I had the mouth of an evil person, and all I could do was fix my gaze on the sweet and serious head I hadn't caressed in so long.

When I left, it seemed as if I had always imagined him that way, so quiet behind his round, blue eyes.

After catching me in front of the mirror several times, Mother urged me to stop trying to find the prettiest way to put up my hair, and consent to having it cut. I didn't have to try too hard to persuade Susana to join me. It was enough to tell her my plans for her to show interest in something that might ultimately benefit her.

When we left the salon, we could hardly disguise our delight. The new haircut softened the reddish tone of my hair, and had a startling effect on Susana's, too. We would have liked not to delay for a moment the surprise and excitement we would cause at home, but an unforeseen encounter thwarted our eagerness: as we went through the gate, we bumped into the gardener.

Immense, brawny, and aging, his hands were enormous and his fingers three times as long and as thick as ours. Each morning when he greeted Susana and me, he would rest his middle finger on one of our shoulders, and this apparently careless gesture alone was enough to urge us forward, to make us stumble if we were caught off guard.

Determined to avoid him, I tried to hide behind one of the gateposts, while Susana ran toward the house. My strategy was as unsuccessful as hers. The gardener crossed her path, bid her good morning, and gave her a prod on the shoulder with his extraordinary finger. Resigned to going through with the unavoidable ritual, I decided to face him immediately.

He looked at me with an air of indecision as if all of a sudden I were less familiar, then held out his hand, and, without touching me, pointed at me with his index finger. For a moment I waited for him to punctuate his greeting with the usual prod, until I understood that he would never do it again.

As I stood motionless before him, my feeling of emptiness grew and grew. I seemed to be drifting away from all I had been until then, and the finger, as it stretched toward me, seemed to point to something unknown, something that, little by little, I was to enter into; something that, as it offered me other emotions and other risks, would gradually separate me from all of those tiny incidents, all of those tiny fears, all my obsessions . . . from all of the tenderness with which my childhood was filled.

TRANSLATOR'S NOTE

When she published *Notes from Childhood* in 1937, it was clear to many that Norah Lange had come into her own as a writer. Leaving behind her prose poetry of the ultraist school, she had begun to claim prose as her territory more fully, and to mine her own life more transparently for her subject matter. Though her earlier prose works, *35 días y 40 marineros* (*35 Days and 40 Sailors*) and the epistolary *Voz de la vida* (*The Voice of Life*), had drawn on her experiences, *Notes from Childhood* embraced a kind of life-writing the author had so far only skirted. It also served as a laboratory for the direction she would later take in her fiction.

The writing of memoir and autobiography in Argentina had been mostly dominated by male voices. *Notes from Childhood* could hardly be further in tone from the kind of autobiography that dwells on history and accomplishments – the official story. Instead, Lange developed a voice that plumbed the depths of domestic life. Historical events and the public sphere encroach only occasionally on this space in the form of official tributes to Lange's father after his death, or a brief glimpse of the Argentine response to the First World War. In her approach to memory, and in training her gaze on domestic, family scenes, the narrator of *Notes from Childhood* shows kinship with the young female narrator of the later novel, *People in the Room*, who writes of the three women across the way from her house that she is drawn to them because "[t]hey seemed to me like the beginning of an accidental life story, without greatness, without photograph albums or display cabinets, but telling meticulously of dresses with stories behind them, of faded letters addressed to other people, of the kind of indelible first portraits that are never forgotten." It is these private, intimate moments that the narrator of Lange's memoir seeks to illuminate in her fragmentary account of the most indelible moments of childhood. Far from being a linear autobiography or tale of coming of age, this narrative takes the form of a constellation of pieces of childhood, and these pieces provide Lange with ground for experimentation.

Notes from Childhood was well received and garnered for its author the Primer Premio de la Provincia de Buenos Aires (the Province of Buenos Aires First Prize) and the Tercer Premio Nacional (Third National Prize), and continues to be Lange's most widely read work in Argentina. But Sylvia Molloy has suggested that the reason Lange's memoir was successful and enduring was not due to her inventive style but because it allowed readers to identify the unconventional Lange with the traditionally feminine subjects of domesticity and childhood. Lange was an eccentric, and until then some critics hadn't been sure where to place her – her account of a journey she took to Norway by boat with forty sailors, for example, was deemed inappropriate for a young woman. By celebrating the charm of the book's subject matter, critics of the period may have overlooked the innovative nature of Lange's prose.

In her brilliant book *At Face Value: Autobiographical Writing in Spanish America*, Molloy describes Lange's project as "a game of cutouts" and her memoir as guided by an "aesthetics of collage." A fragment of *Notes* describing schoolroom activities shows us the young Lange snipping words from newspaper headlines: "With a pair of scissors, I would clip words from the local and foreign papers, arranging them into little piles. Most of the time, I didn't know what they meant, but I didn't mind this at all. What drew me in was the typeface, the thick and thin strokes of the script." Lange identifies this as one of the earliest instances in which she experienced "aesthetic" pleasure.

It was with *Notes from Childhood* that Lange claimed prose as her ground for stylistic innovation. Lange portrays herself as a fearful child, assailed by multiple obsessions. While the games she plays may be viewed as typical of childhood, in her retelling of them, the author turns them into an aesthetic strategy. Her anxious playfulness reaches an extreme in her game of entering the profiles of the people she meets, viewing their faces from within, contorting her body like an acrobat to fit inside them. Here we are closer to the limitless childhood imagination celebrated by surrealism than to a sentimental portrayal of domestic life.

Lange was no stranger to the numerous movements that shaped European and Latin American modernism, and was surely familiar with collage and its relationship to cubism. The ultraist movement imported from Spain by Borges, of which Lange's book of poems *La calle de la tarde* (*The Street at Dusk*) is considered an example, was influenced by cubism, dadaism, expressionism, and futurism. (Marinetti famously visited Buenos Aires in 1926; Norah was slated to read him one of her poems, but her inhibition made it necessary for a friend to read on her behalf.) She had been steeped in the avant-garde milieu since she was a teenager. With the poet Oliverio Girondo, whom she later married, and a cadre of contemporaries, she waged a "war on solemnity," collaborating on the earliest journals of the Argentine avant-garde, participating in raucous dadaist happenings, and performing the speeches she wrote at an endless stream of banquets. Norah later recalled that she gave her speeches standing on a crate of wine, since she liked to "dominate the crowd." In the speech she penned in honor of the Lange family and performed at the banquet celebrating the publication of *Notes from Childhood*, she recalled the *tertulias* that used to take place at the house on Calle Tronador, where Jorge Luis Borges listened to old tangos, while Horacio Quiroga and Alfonsina Storni played parlor games, Leopoldo Marechal discussed "poetic possibilities" with his contemporaries, Macedonio Fernández sauntered through in a poncho and Ramón Gómez de la Serna in a pinstripe suit, and the painter Xul Solar "translated troubling horoscopes into seventeen languages." Solar spent over a decade in Europe, where he met the painter Emilio Pettoruti, whose cubist exhibition was inaugurated in 1924 on his return to Buenos Aires, and is considered a watershed moment in the *vanguardia*. That same year, the journal *Martín Fierro,* to which Norah became a contributor, was launched. The magazine's manifesto positioned it in opposition to "the funereal solemnity of the historian and academic, who mummifies all he touches." These were years of intense intellectual and artistic ferment in the Argentine capital, and many of the connections vital to this were forged at the legendary *tertulias* in the Lange family home.

Early in *Notes from Childhood*, the narrator recalls an often-repeated scene in which her parents would mount their horses in front of the family home, then ride off into the distance as their children looked on. The daughter describes the strange visual effect of her mother riding side-saddle in a long, old-fashioned riding habit. On one side, visible to the children as they look on, is the "whole length" of their mother, "the black brim of her hat concealing her face." On the other side, they see "only a single gloved hand," but "her profile was as sharp as if she had suddenly drawn alongside a lamp." To the narrator, the two sides, light and dark, visible and concealed, one "shadowy, mysterious," one "whole" and "intact," appear to balance each other out, yet for the reader (and the translator) the image is hard to visualize; it takes imaginative work to occupy the narrator's perspective, to conjure these two sides of the mother before our eyes. What we have to work with are light and shadow, a profile, outlines, in order to inhabit her daughters' experience of this game of concealment and revelation.

Partial views, oblique angles, and challenging images are essential to Lange's prose, and in her memoir she found ample terrain for experimentation. The nameless narrator views scenes from childhood through her mother, father, and sister's windows; she spies on a sister while hiding behind a door; she fantasizes about surreptitious glimpses of her French teacher's daughter through a crack. Such perspectives are ideal for exploring a child's partial understanding of her surroundings and of the adult world, and also for testing the parameters of modernist imagery. In Lange's memoir, the gazing subject's view is often obstructed or mediated by something other than its object: the narrator speaks of the "poplars that so many times sliced through our view." On a journey, the blanket keeping the children warm is "a still strip of shadow slicing the cart horizontally in two." Beside the Christmas tree, her sisters' faces are "happy triangles briefly glimpsed through a gap in the branches." When Marta covers her face in misery when their father teaches her to tell the time, her sisters glimpse bits of her face through her outspread fingers, "a moistened eye, a patch of nose, a corner of mouth," as if Lange had clipped the face into its components and reassembled them as a cubist painting. This mediation contributes to an aesthetic that can be likened to that of the tendencies explored by Lange's contemporaries in the visual arts.

In the years preceding the publication of Lange's memoir, the photographer Horacio Coppola made a series of photographs of Buenos Aires that became fundamental to the Argentine capital's concept of itself as a modern city. His photographs appeared frequently in the journal *Sur*, and illustrated Borges's *Evaristo Carriego*, in 1930. Coppola became famous for his documentation of urban life and for chronicling Buenos Aires architecture, and played a part in the modernist aesthetic renovation underway in all aspects of artistic culture. His photographs shot from balconies looking onto the street below, and from all manner of oblique angles, are a prime example of the kind of experimentation with perspective that was common to the period. Photographs such as *Medianera con aire y luz* (Wall with Air and Light) and *Toldos* (Awnings), both from 1931, position the gaze at an unusual angle. In photographs such as these, I found not only a viewing subject analogous to Lange as a child, but an aesthetic of the fleeting that informed some of my translation choices. New visual technologies are often present in Lange's work: in family photographs, in the scene where the protagonist's sisters have their first-communion portraits taken, in the silent film the girls are finally allowed to see at the local cinema. In this last case, the silent film seems to provide a key to viewing a reality that supersedes it: after the young Norah sees the film, it is the sight of the horse with a dead man over its rump that provides the more enduring image: "My memory of the first film we ever saw is always shot through with that of a lone man on the road to the town cemetery." It was this consideration of the photographic in Lange's work that finally led me to translate the book's first word, *entrecortado*, as "flickering," images recovered through the flickering of a screen, or viewed through a stereoscope as it comes into focus. In *People in the Room*, the connection becomes more explicit, when the young female narrator writes of her habit of gazing through the window at the women across the street, "It was as if I was slowly composing a silent film that might go on forever," the narrator-viewer manipulating scenes from behind an imagined camera.

My first image of Lange, when I learned of her work ten years ago, came from Edwin Williamson's biography of Jorge Luis

Borges. Here, Lange is depicted as a gregarious, flame-haired tomboy who used to bedevil her neighbors by laughing and shrieking and throwing things from the rooftops. Williamson's account of Lange's friendship with Borges furthers the narrative that contributed to her enshrinement in literary history as muse of the Argentine avant-garde. The image of the enigmatic Lange making a spectacle of herself on the roof originates in one of the most striking fragments of *Notes from Childhood*, where Lange describes the routine she developed in adolescence of climbing onto the kitchen roof of Calle Tronador, wrapped in a poncho and donning a man's felt hat. She would summon the neighbors by name, regaling them with a string of "expletives . . . paragraphs in English and French, disjointed sentences . . . the few words I knew in Italian or Norwegian, collective insults, a raucous guffaw, an affected line of verse." This is not the behavior of a passive muse but of a young woman testing the power of her voice. Here we see the seed of the self-possession and the instinct to act that would result in Lange's dadaist banquet speeches. As Lange peers from the kitchen roof into the surrounding houses, we catch a glimpse of the spy casting her furtive glances from above, positioning herself as viewing subject but also as subject on view. The collagist manipulating her materials from behind the scenes has also become a performer, making the transformation from obsessive child into self-conscious narrator almost complete.

CHARLOTTE WHITTLE,
BROOKLYN, JANUARY 2021

Dear readers,

As well as relying on bookshop sales, And Other Stories relies on subscriptions from people like you for many of our books, whose stories other publishers often consider too risky to take on.

Our subscribers don't just make the books physically happen. They also help us approach booksellers, because we can demonstrate that our books already have readers and fans. And they give us the security to publish in line with our values, which are collaborative, imaginative and 'shamelessly literary'.

All of our subscribers:

- receive a first-edition copy of each of the books they subscribe to
- are thanked by name at the end of our subscriber-supported books
- receive little extras from us by way of thank you, for example: postcards created by our authors

BECOME A SUBSCRIBER, OR GIVE A SUBSCRIPTION TO A FRIEND

Visit andotherstories.org/subscriptions to help make our books happen. You can subscribe to books we're in the process of making. To purchase books we have already published, we urge you to support your local or favourite bookshop and order directly from them – the often unsung heroes of publishing.

OTHER WAYS TO GET INVOLVED

If you'd like to know about upcoming events and reading groups (our foreign-language reading groups help us choose books to publish, for example) you can:

- join our mailing list at: andotherstories.org
- follow us on Twitter: @andothertweets
- join us on Facebook: facebook.com/AndOtherStoriesBooks
- admire our books on Instagram: @andotherpics
- follow our blog: andotherstories.org/ampersand

This book was made possible thanks to the support of:

A Cudmore
Aaron McEnery
Aaron Schneider
Abel Gonzalez
Abigail Howell
Abigail Walton
Ada Gokay
Adam Lenson
Adrian Astur Alvarez
Adrian Perez
Adriana Diaz Enciso
Adriana Francisco
Aifric Campbell
Ailsa Peate
Aisha McLean
Ajay Sharma
Alan Baldwin
Alan Donnelly
Alan Hunter
Alan McMonagle
Alan Stoskopf
Alastair Gillespie
Alastair Whitson
Alecia Marshall
Alex Hoffman
Alex Lockwood
Alex Ramsey
Alex Robertson
Alexander Barbour
Alexander Leggatt
Alexandra Citron
Alexandra Stewart
Alexandra Stewart
Alexandra Tilden
Alfred Birnbaum
Ali Riley
Ali Smith
Ali Usman
Alice Morgan
Alice Shumate
Alice Smith

Alice Wilkinson
Alison Layland
Alison Winston
Aliya Rashid
Allison LaSorda
Alyse Ceirante
Alyssa Rinaldi
Alyssa Tauber
Amado Floresca
Amaia Gabantxo
Amanda
Amanda Astley
Amanda Dalton
Amanda Geenen
Amanda Maria
  Izquierdo Gonzalez
Amanda Read
Amber Da
Amelia Lowe
Amine Hamadache
Amy and Jamie
Amy Bessent
Amy Bojang
Andra Dusu
Andrea Barlien
Andrea Brownstone
Andrea Reece
Andrew Kerr-Jarrett
Andrew Marston
Andrew McCallum
Andrew Rego
Andy Corsham
Andy Marshall
Angela Everitt
Angelica Ribichini
Ann Menzies
Anna-Maria Aurich
Anna Dowrick
Anna Finneran
Anna Gibson
Anna Hawthorne

Anna Milsom
Anna Zaranko
Anne Barnes
Anne Boileau Clarke
Anne Carus
Anne Craven
Anne Edyvean
Anne Frost
Anne Guest
Anne Magnier-Redon
Anne-Marie Renshaw
Anne Sticksel
Anne Stokes
Anne Willborn
Anonymous
Anonymous
Anthony Alexander
Anthony Brown
Anthony Cotton
Anthony Quinn
Antonia Lloyd-Jones
Antonia Saske
Antony Pearce
Aoife Boyd
Archie Davies
Arthur John Rowles
Asako Serizawa
Ashleigh Sutton
Ashley Cairns
Audrey Mash
Audrey Small
Barbara Bettsworth
Barbara Mellor
Barbara Robinson
Barbara Spicer
Barbara Wheatley
Barry John Fletcher
Barry Norton
Barry Watkinson
Bea Karol Burks
Ben Schofield

Ben Sharratt
Ben Thornton
Ben Walter
Ben Wormald
Benjamin Judge
Benjamin Pester
Bethlehem Attfield
Beverley Thomas
Bhakti Gajjar
Bianca Duec
Bianca Jackson
Bianca Winter
Bill Fletcher
Birgitta Karlén
Bjørnar Djupevik
   Hagen
Blazej Jedras
Brendan Monroe
Briallen Hopper
Brian Anderson
Brian Byrne
Brian Callaghan
Brian Smith
Brigita Ptackova
Brooke Williams
Burkhard Fehsenfeld
Caitlin Halpern
Caitriona Lally
Cal Smith
Callie Steven
Cam Scott
Cameron Adams
Camilla Imperiali
Campbell McEwan
Carl Emery
Carla Castanos
Carol Mavor
Carole Burns
Carolina Pineiro
Caroline Jupp
Caroline Smith
Caroline West
Carrie Allen
Cassidy Hughes

Catharine
   Braithwaite
Catherine Cleary
Catherine Fearns
Catherine Lambert
Catherine Tolo
Catherine
   Williamson
Catie Kosinski
Catriona Gibbs
Cecilia Cerrini
Cecilia Rossi
Cecilia Uribe
Ceri Webb
Chantal Wright
Charlene Huggins
Charles Dee Mitchell
Charles Fernyhough
Charles Kovach
Charles Raby
Charles Tocock
Charlie Errock
Charlotte Briggs
Charlotte Holtam
Charlotte Middleton
Charlotte Ryland
Charlotte Whittle
Charlotte Woodford
Chelsey Johnson
Chenxin Jiang
Cherilyn Elston
Cherise Wolas
China Miéville
Chloe Baird
Chris Gostick
Chris Gribble
Chris Holmes
Chris Köpruner
Chris Lintott
Chris Potts
Chris Stevenson
Chris Thornton
Christian
   Schuhmann

Christina Moutsou
Christine Bartels
Christine Elliott
Christopher Allen
Christopher Homfray
Christopher Jenkin
Christopher Smith
Christopher Stout
Ciara Ní Riain
Claire Adams
Claire Hayward
Claire Potter
Claire Riley
Claire Williams
Clarice Borges
Clarissa Pattern
Cliona Quigley
Clive Bellingham
Colin Denyer
Colin Hewlett
Colin Matthews
Collin Brooke
Cornelia Svedman
Cortina Butler
Courtney Lilly
Craig Kennedy
Csilla Toldy
Cynthia De La Torre
Cyrus Massoudi
Daisy Savage
Dale Wisely
Dana Lapidot
Daniel Arnold
Daniel Coxon
Daniel Gillespie
Daniel Hahn
Daniel Jàrmai
Daniel Jones
Daniel Oudshoorn
Daniel Stewart
Daniel Wood
Daniela Steierberg
Darina Brejtrova
Darren Davies

Dave Lander
David Anderson
David Coates
David Cowan
David Davies
David Greenlaw
David Gunnarsson
David Hebblethwaite
David Higgins
David Hodges
David Kendall
David Key
David Leverington
David F Long
David McIntyre
David Miller
David Miller
David Reid
David Richardson
David Shriver
David Smith
David Thornton
Davis MacMillan
Dawn Bass
Dean Stokes
Dean Taucher
Debbie Pinfold
Deborah Banks
Declan Gardner
Declan O'Driscoll
Deirdre Nic
    Mhathuna
Denis Larose
Denis Stillewagt &
    Anca Fronescu
Denton Djurasevich
Derek Taylor-
    Vrsalovich
Desiree Mason
Detta Eldor
Diana Baker Smith
Diana Digges
Diane Salisbury
Dimitra Kolliakou

Dinesh Prasad
Dipika Mummery
Dirk Hanson
Dominic Nolan
Dominick Santa
    Cattarina
Dominique Brocard
Drew Gummerson
Duncan Clubb
Duncan Macgregor
Duncan Marks
Dustin Haviv
Dyanne Prinsen
E Rodgers
Earl James
Ebba Aquila
Ebba Tornérhielm
Ed Tronick
Ekaterina Beliakova
Elena Galindo
Elif Aganoglu
Elina Zicmane
Elisabeth Cook
Elizabeth Braswell
Elizabeth Cochrane
Elizabeth Dillon
Elizabeth Draper
Elizabeth Franz
Elizabeth Leach
Elizabeth Perry
Elizabeth Seal
Ellen Beardsworth
Ellen Casey
Emeline Morin
Emily McCarthy
Emily Walker
Emily Webber
Emma Barraclough
Emma Bielecki
Emma Coulson
Emma Dell
Emma Louise Grove
Emma Page
Emma Post

Emma Teale
Ena Lee
Eric Anderson
Eric Cassells
Eric Reinders
Eric Tucker
Erin Cameron Allen
Esmée de Heer
Esther Donnelly
Etta Searle
Eugene O'Hare
Eunji Kim
Eva Mitchell
Eva Oddo
Eve Corcoran
Ewan Tant
F Gary Knapp
Fay Barrett
Faye Williams
Felix Valdivieso
Finbarr Farragher
Fiona Davenport
    White
Fiona Liddle
Fiona Quinn
Florian Duijsens
Fran Sanderson
Frances
    Christodoulou
Frances Thiessen
Frances Winfield
Francesca Brooks
Francesca Rhydderch
Francis Mathias
Frank van Orsouw
Frankie Mullin
Fred Nichols
Freddie Radford
Freya Killilea-Clark
Friederike Knabe
Gabriel Colnic
Gabriel and Mary de
    Courcy Cooney
Gala Copley

Garan Holcombe
Gareth Tulip
Gary Gorton
Gavin Smith
Gawain Espley
Gemma Bird
Genaro Palomo Jr
Geoff Thrower
Geoffrey Cohen
Geoffrey Urland
George McCaig
George Stanbury
Georgia Panteli
Georgia Shomidie
Georgina Hildick-
   Smith
Georgina Norton
Gerry Craddock
Gill Boag-Munroe
Gillian Grant
Gillian Spencer
Gordon Cameron
Gosia Pennar
Graham Blenkinsop
Graham R Foster
Grant Rintoul
Gregory Philp
Hadil Balzan
Hamish Russell
Hanna Varady &
   Mikael Awake
Hannah Bucknell
Hannah Davies
Hannah Freeman
Hannah Jane
   Lownsbrough
Hannah Procter
Hannah Rapley
Hannah Vidmark
Hanora Bagnell
Hans Lazda
Harriet Stiles
Harry Plant
Haydon Spenceley

Heather & Andrew
   Ordover
Heidi Gilhooly
Helen Berry
Helen Brady
Helen Coombes
Helen Moor
Helen Wilson
Helena Buffery
Henriette
   Magerstaedt
Henry Bell
Henry Patino
Holly Barker
Holly Down
Howard Robinson
Hugh Shipley
Hyoung-Won Park
Iain Munro
Ian Hagues
Ian McMillan
Ian Mond
Ida Grochowska
Ifer Moore
Ilona Abb
Ingunn Vallumroed
Iona Preston
Irene Croal
Irene Mansfield
Irina Tzanova
Isabel Adey
Isabella Livorni
Isabella Weibrecht
Isobel Foxford
JC Blake
J Drew Hancock-Teed
Jacinta Perez Gavilan
   Torres
Jack Brown
Jack Williams
Jacob Blizard
Jacqueline Lademann
Jacqueline Ting Lin
Jacqui Hudson

Jacqui Jackson
Jade Yiu
Jadie Lee
Jake Baldwinson
James Avery
James Beck
James Crossley
James Cubbon
James Dahm
James Kinsley
James Lee
James Lehmann
James Leonard
James Lesniak
James Mewis
James Norman
James Portlock
James Scudamore
James Ward
Jamie Cox
Jamie Mollart
Jamie Veitch
Jamie Walsh
Jan Hicks
Jane Anderton
Jane Bryce
Jane Dolman
Jane Fairweather
Jane Leuchter
Jane Roberts
Jane Roberts
Jane Woollard
Janet Kofi-Tsekpo
Janne Støen
Jasmine Gideon
Jason Grunebaum
Jason Lever
Jason Sim
Jason Timermanis
Jayne Watson
Jeff Collins
Jeffrey Davies
Jenifer Logie
Jennifer Arnold

Jennifer Fisher
Jennifer Harvey
Jennifer Higgins
Jennifer Mills
Jennifer Watts
Jenny Barlow
Jenny Huth
Jenny Newton
Jeremy Koenig
Jeremy Morton
Jeremy Wellens
Jerry Simcock
Jess Hazlewood
Jesse Coleman
Jesse Hara
Jesse Thayre
Jessica Kibler
Jessica Laine
Jessica Martin
Jessica Queree
Jessica Weetch
Jethro Soutar
Jill Harrison
Jill Oliver
Jo Elliot
Joanna Luloff
Joanne Smith
Joao Pedro Bragatti
    Winckler
JoDee Brandon
Jodie Adams
Joe Gill
Joel Swerdlow
Johanna Eliasson
Johannes Holmqvist
Johannes Menzel
John Bennett
John Berube
John Bogg
John Carnahan
John Conway
John Down
John Gent
John Hanson

John Higginson
John Hodgson
John Kelly
John Royley
John Shaw
John Steigerwald
John Walsh
John Winkelman
Jon Riches
Jon Talbot
Jonathan Blaney
Jonathan Fiedler
Jonathan Huston
Jonathan Ruppin
Jonny Kiehlmann
Jordana Carlin
Jose Machado
Joseph Darlington
Joseph Flading
Joseph Novak
Joseph Schreiber
Josephine Glöckner
Josh Calvo
Josh Sumner
Joshua Davis
Joshua McNamara
Joy Paul
Judith Austin
Judith Gruet-Kaye
Judy Davies
Judy Lee-Fenton
Judy Tomlinson
Julia Von Dem
    Knesebeck
Julia Shmotkina
Julian Hemming
Julian Molina
Julie Greenwalt
Julie Hutchinson
Julie Winter
Julienne van Loon
Juliet Birkbeck
Juliet Swann
Juraj Janik

Justine Goodchild
K Elkes
Kaarina Hollo
Kaelyn Davis
Kaja R Anker-Rasch
Kasper Haakansson
Kat Côté
Kataline Lukacs
Kate Attwooll
Kate Beswick
Kate Gardner
Kate Procter
Kate Shires
Katharina Liehr
Katharine Freeman
Katharine Robbins
Katherine Mackinnon
Kathryn Edwards
Kathryn Hemmann
Kathryn Oliver
Kathryn Williams
Kathy Gogarty
Katia Wengraf
Katie Brown
Katie Grant
Katie Kennedy
Katie Kline
Katie Smart
Katy Robinson
Katy West
Kayleigh Dray
Keith Walker
Kennedy McCullough
Kenneth Blythe
Kenneth Michaels
Kent McKernan
Kerry Parke
Kieran Rollin
Kieron James
Kim McGowan
Kim Metcalf
Kira Josefsson
Kirsten Hey
Kirsty Doole

Kirsty Simpkins
Klara Rešetič
Kris Ann Trimis
Kristen Tcherneshoff
Kristin Djuve
Krystale Tremblay-
  Moll
Krystine Phelps
Kysanna Shawney
Lacy Wolfe
Lana Selby
Lara Vergnaud
Laura Batatota
Laura Clarke
Laura Ling
Laura Pugh
Laura Rangeley
Laura Zederkof
Lauren Pout
Lauren Schluneger
Laurence Laluyaux
Laury Leite
Leah Zamesnik
Leanne Radojkovich
Lee Harbour
Leeanne Parker
Leelynn Brady
Leon Geis
Leonora Randall
Liliana Lobato
Lily Blacksell
Lily Robert-Foley
Lindsay Attree
Lindsay Brammer
Lindsey Ford
Linette Arthurton
  Bruno
Lisa Agostini
Lisa Bean
Lisa Dillman
Lisa Fransson
Lisa Leahigh
Lisa Simpson
Lisa Tomlinson

Lisa Weizenegger
Liz Clifford
Liz Ketch
Lorna Bleach
Lottie Smith
Louise Evans
Louise Greenberg
Louise Hoelscher
Louise Smith
Louise Whittaker
Luc Verstraete
Lucas J Medeiros
Lucia Rotheray
Lucie Taylor
Lucile Lesage
Lucy Beevor
Lucy Greaves
Lucy Moffatt
Ludmilla Jordanova
Luke Loftiss
Lydia Trethewey
Lynda Graham
Lynn Fung
Lynn Martin
Lynn Ross
M Manfre
Madeline Teevan
Maeve Lambe
Magdaline Rohweder
Maggie Humm
Maggie Redway
Mahan L Ellison & K
  Ashley Dickson
Malgorzata Rokicka
Mandy Wight
Marcel Schlamowitz
Margaret Dillow
Maria Ahnhem Farrar
Maria Lomunno
Maria Losada
Maria Pia Tissot
Marie Cloutier
Marie Donnelly
Marijana Rimac

Marina Castledine
Marina Galanti
Marina Jones
Mario Sifuentez
Marisa Wilson
Mark Harris
Mark Huband
Mark Sargent
Mark Scott
Mark Sheets
Mark Sztyber
Mark Waters
Marlene Adkins
Marlene Simoes
Martha Nicholson
Martha Stevns
Martin Brown
Martin Nathan
Mary Heiss
Mary Ellen Nagle
Mary Nash
Mary Wang
Mathias Ruthner
Mathilde Pascal
Matt Davies
Matt Greene
Matt O'Connor
Matteo Besana
Matthew Adamson
Matthew Armstrong
Matthew Black
Matthew Francis
Matthew Gill
Matthew Lowe
Matthew Scott
Matthew Warshauer
Matthew Woodman
Maura Cheeks
Maureen Pritchard
Max Cairnduff
Max Garrone
Max Longman
Max McCabe
Maya Chung

Meaghan Delahunt
Meg Lovelock
Megan Wittling
Meghan Goodeve
Melissa Beck
Melissa Quignon-
  Finch
Melissa Stogsdill
Melissa Wan
Meredith Jones
Meredith Martin
Meryl Wingfield
Michael Bichko
Michael Dodd
Michael James
  Eastwood
Michael Friddle
Michael Gavin
Michael Holt
Michael Kuhn
Michael Moran
Michael Pollak
Michael Roess
Michael
  Schneiderman
Miguel Head
Mike Turner
Mildred Nicotera
Milla Rautio
Miranda Gold
Miriam McBride
Mona Arshi
Moray Teale
Morgan Lyons
Moshe Prigan
Muireann Maguire
Myka Tucker-
  Abramson
Myles Nolan
Myna Trustram
N Tsolak
Nan Craig
Nancy Jacobson
Nancy Oakes

Naomi Morauf
Natalie Ricks
Nathalie Atkinson
Nathalie Karagiannis
Nathan McNamara
Nathan Weida
Neferti Tadiar
Nguyen Phan
Nicholas Brown
Nicholas Rutherford
Nicholas Smith
Nick Chapman
Nick James
Nick Love
Nick Nelson & Rachel
  Eley
Nick Sidwell
Nick Twemlow
Nicola Cook
Nicola Hart
Nicola Mira
Nicola Sandiford
Nicola Scott
Nicole Matteini
Nicoletta Asciuto
Nigel Fishburn
Niki Sammut
Nikki Dudley
Nina Alexandersen
Niven Kumar
Odilia Corneth
Olga Alexandru
Olga Zilberbourg
Olivia Payne
Órla Ní Chuilleanáin
  and Dónall Ó
  Ceallaigh
Pamela Ritchie
Pamela Tao
Patrick Hawley
Patrick Hoare
Patrick McGuinness
Paul Brackenridge
Paul Cray

Paul Jones
Paul Munday
Paul Myatt
Paul Scott
Paul Segal
Paula Edwards
Paula Turner
Pauline France
Pavlos Stavropoulos
Paz Berlese
Penelope Hewett
  Brown
Perlita Payne
Peter Hudson
Peter Van de Maele
  and Narina Dahms
Peter McBain
Peter McCambridge
Peter Rowland
Peter Taplin
Peter Watson
Peter Wells
Petra Stapp
Phil Bartlett
Philip Herbert
Philip Warren
Philip Williams
Philipp Jarke
Phillipa Clements
Phoebe McKenzie
Phoebe Millerwhite
Piet Van Bockstal
PRAH Foundation
Prakash Nayak
Priya Sharma
Rachael de Moravia
Rachael Williams
Rachel Carter
Rachel Dolan
Rachel Van Riel
Rachel Watkins
Ranbir Sidhu
Rebecca Braun
Rebecca Carter

Rebecca Micklewright
Rebecca Moss
Rebecca O'Reilly
Rebecca Parry
Rebecca Rose
Rebecca Rosenthal
Rebecca Shaak
Rebekka Bremmer
Rhiannon Armstrong
Rhodri Jones
Rich Sutherland
Richard Ashcroft
Richard Catty
Richard Dew
Richard Ellis
Richard Gwyn
Richard Harrison
Richard Mansell
Richard Priest
Richard Sanders
Richard Shea
Richard Soundy
Richard White
Rita O'Brien
Robert Gillett
Robert Hamilton
Robert Hannah
Robert Sliman
Robert Wolff
Robin McLean
Robin Taylor
Robina Franko
Rogelio Pardo
Roger Newton
Roger Ramsden
Ronan Cormacain
Rory Williamson
Ros Woolner
Rosalind May
Rosalind Ramsay
Rosanna Foster
Rose Crichton
Roxanne O'Del Ablett

Royston Tester
Roz Simpson
Rupert Ziziros
Ruth Deyermond
Ruth Field
Ryan Day
SK Grout
ST Dabbagh
Sally Baker
Sally Bramley
Sally Hall
Sam Gordon
Sam Reese
Sam Southwood
Samuel Crosby
Sara Kittleson
Sara Sherwood
Sarah Arboleda
Sarah Blunden
Sarah Brewer
Sarah Elizabeth
Sarah Farley
Sarah Forster
Sarah Lucas
Sarah Manvel
Sarah Pybus
Sarah Roff
Sarah Spitz
Sarah Wert
Scott Astrada
Scott Chiddister
Scott Henkle
Scott Russell
Sean McDonagh
Sez Kiss
Shannon Knapp
Sharon Dogar
Sharon McCammon
Shaun Whiteside
Shauna Gilligan
Shauna Rogers
Sheila Duffy
Sheila Packa
Sheryl Jermyn

Shira Lob
Shona Holmes
Sian Hannah
Sienna Kang
Simon Clark
Simon Gray
Simon Pitney
Simon Robertson
Sonia McLintock
Sophia Wickham
Sophie Rees
Soren Murhart
Stacy Rodgers
Stefanie Schrank
Stefano Mula
Stephan Eggum
Stephanie Lacava
Stephanie Laurindo Da Silva
Stephanie Shields
Stephen Cunliffe
Stephen Eisenhammer
Stephen Pearsall
Steve Chapman
Steve James
Steve Raby
Steven & Gitte Evans
Steven Norton
Steven E Sanderson
Steven Vass
Steven Willborn
Stu Hennigan
Stu Sherman
Stuart Grey
Stuart Snelson
Stuart Wilkinson
Su Bonfanti
Subhashree Beeman
Sunny Payson
Susan Edsall
Susan Jaken
Susan Winter
Sylvie Zannier-Betts

Tamara Larsen
Tamsin Walker
Tara Pahari
Tara Roman
Tasmin Maitland
Taylor Ffitch
Teresa Werner
Teri Hoskin
Tessa Lang
The Mighty Douche
  Softball Team
Therese Oulton
Thom Cuell
Thom Keep
Thomas van den Bout
Thomas Fritz
Thomas Mitchell
Thomas Rasmussen
Thomas Smith
Thomas Andrew
  White
Tian Zheng
Tiffany Lehr
Tim Kelly
Tim Scott
Tim Theroux

Tina Rotherham-
  Winqvist
Toby Halsey
Toby Ryan
Tom Darby
Tom Doyle
Tom Franklin
Tom Gray
Tom Stafford
Tom Whatmore
Tony Bastow
Tory Jeffay
Tracy Bauld
Tracy Heuring
Tracy Lee-Newman
Tracy Northup
Trevor Wald
Val Challen
Valerie O'Riordan
Vanessa Dodd
Vanessa Fuller
Vanessa Heggie
Vanessa Nolan
Vanessa Rush
Veronica Barnsley
Victor Meadowcroft

Victoria Eld
Victoria Goodbody
Victoria Huggins
Vijay Pattisapu
Vikki O'Neill
Wendy Langridge
Wendy Olson
William
  Brockenborough
William Dennehy
William Franklin
William Schwaber
William Schwartz
William Sitters
William Wood
Xanthe Rendall
Yaseen Khan
Yasmin Alam
Zachary Hope
Zachary Maricondia
Zara Rahman
Zezinha De Senha
Zoe Thomas
Zoë Brasier

Born in 1905 to Norwegian parents in Buenos Aires, NORAH LANGE was a key figure in the Argentine avant-garde of the early to mid-twentieth century. Though she began her career writing poetry, her first major success came in 1937 with her memoir *Notes from Childhood*, followed by the companion memoir *Antes que mueran* (*Before They Die*), and the novels *People in the Room* and *Los dos retratos* (*The Two Portraits*). She contributed to the magazines *Proa* and *Martín Fierro*, and was a friend to figures such as Jorge Luis Borges, Pablo Neruda, and Federico García Lorca. From her teenage years, when her family home became the site of many literary gatherings, Norah was at the heart of Buenos Aires' literary scene. She traveled widely alone and with her husband, always returning to Buenos Aires, where she continued to write and host literary gatherings. She died in 1972.

CHARLOTTE WHITTLE has translated works by Jorge Comensal, Agus Morales, and Elisa Victoria, among others, and was instrumental in bringing the work of Norah Lange to audiences in English. Her translation of Lange's *People in the Room* was longlisted for the Best Translated Book Award and shortlisted for both the Warwick Prize for Women in Translation and the Society of Authors' TA First Translation Prize. Her work on *Notes from Childhood* won a PEN Translates award. She lives in New York.